Cambridge
checkpoint

Lower Secondary
World English
9

Fiona Macgregor
Daphne Paizee
EDUCATIONAL CONSULTANT:
Sioban Parker

HODDER EDUCATION
AN HACHETTE UK COMPANY

Registered Cambridge International Schools benefit from high-quality programmes, assessments and a wide range of support so that teachers can effectively deliver Cambridge Lower Secondary. Visit www.cambridgeinternational.org/lowersecondary to find out more.

Third-party websites and resources referred to in this publication have not been endorsed by Cambridge Assessment International Education.

The authors would like to thank Susan Kelly for her excellent input and guidance while developing this material, and Rebecca Norman for her diligent and conscientious editing.

Audio files are free to download at www.hoddereducation.com/cambridgeextras

Orders: please contact Bookpoint Ltd, 130 Park Drive, Milton Park, Abingdon, Oxon OX14 4SE. Telephone: +44 (0)1235 827827. Fax: +44 (0)1235 400401. Email: education@bookpoint.co.uk Lines are open from 9 a.m. to 5 p.m., Monday to Saturday, with a 24-hour message answering service. You can also order through our website: www.hoddereducation.com

ISBN: 9781398311435

First published in 2021 by

Hodder Education
An Hachette UK Company
Carmelite House
50 Victoria Embankment
London EC4Y 0DZ
www.hoddereducation.com

Impression number 10 9 8 7 6 5 4 3 2 1

Year 2025 2024 2023 2022 2021

Illustration by Barking Dog Art and The Bright Group International

Typeset in FS Albert 12/14pt by Ian Foulis Design, Saltash, Cornwall

Printed in Italy

A catalogue record for this title is available from the British Library.

FSC www.fsc.org MIX Paper from responsible sources FSC™ C104740

Contents

Introduction

How can English help you in your everyday life and connect you to the exciting and challenging world in which we live? In *Cambridge Checkpoint Lower Secondary World English,* we encourage you to connect to this world by thinking and reflecting as you learn.

We have provided topics for a variety of different interests, from living in remote areas to using social media and making business plans. You will have the opportunity to use the new language that you learn to share ideas and learn from others too. This will help you to become confident and fluent in English. The language and the skills that you learn will also help you in other subjects.

This series therefore helps you to access your world and to stay connected to it. Be the best that you can and become a responsible and thinking citizen of the world.

Enjoy your learning experience!

Daphne Paizee
Fiona Macgregor

How to use this book

To make your study of Cambridge Lower Secondary English as a Second Language (0876) as rewarding as possible, look out for the following features when you are using this book:

- These aims show you what you will be covering in the unit.

PRACTISE
Activities that help you to put new skills, information and knowledge to practical use.

Try this

These questions help you to develop skills, knowledge and comprehension.

CHALLENGE YOURSELF
These are more demanding tasks or tasks that help you to practise a wider range of skills.

Do you remember?

These provide a quick recap on earlier grammar points and may sometimes include a question.

LET'S TALK
These tasks provide opportunities for more free discussion towards the end of a unit.

DID YOU KNOW?
These contain interesting information or facts.

HINT
Useful points to note or help with an activity.

Self check
Summary questions or tasks that occur at the end of each unit.

What can you do?
This provides an end-of-unit checklist of key content.

This book contains lots of activities to help you learn. Most of these have symbols beside them to help you know what type of activity they are.

This means that there is a listening activity, along with an audio track reference. All audio is available to download for free from www.hoddereducation.com/cambridgeextras

This means that there is a speaking activity. These are different to the Let's Talk boxes, which are freer discussion tasks that usually occur towards the end of a unit.

This tells you that content is related to another subject.

There is a link to digital content at the end of each unit if you are using the Boost eBook.

At the end of this book you will find some additional features to help you while you study.

- The glossary is a list of some words you might not have encountered before, or words that are specific to one of the units you will be studying. If you want to check the meaning of a word you come across in this book, check the glossary. If it's not there, use a dictionary.
- The grammar section includes all the grammar points you will learn throughout this book. It is arranged in alphabetical order so you can find everything easily.
- Check the punctuation chart to remind yourself how to use punctuation accurately in your own writing. This chart will help you understand different forms of punctuation and how to use them properly.
- The pronunciation word bank is a list of interesting words that appear in this book. You might not have heard some of these words before. Listen to the Audio list of these words to learn to pronounce them properly. Read the words as you listen.
- At the back of the book is a list of books you might like to read for enjoyment. Reading is a great way to relax, to use your imagination, and to learn about new people, places and things. Most of all – it's fun!

1 Making a stand

In this unit you will:

- listen to young **activists** talk about providing electricity for their community and getting rid of plastic waste
- give your opinions about young activists who are trying to change the world, and talk about your own solutions for a problem your community faces
- read letters about a **protest** that a president got involved in, and a newspaper article about an activist providing relevant books for black girls
- write a letter to a well-known person asking for support for your **campaign**
- use a range of future active and passive forms, future continuous forms and present perfect continuous forms.

▲ Meet Marley Dias, who started the #1000blackgirlbooks organisation

▲ Kelvin Doe, a.k.a. DJ Focus, is a self-trained engineer from Sierra Leone, who built his own batteries and a generator from scrap materials he found in garbage heaps

Speaking and listening

Focus on the future

Meet some of the clever young people who are bringing change to our world. Look at the photographs on the opposite page. Read the captions carefully.

Discuss the photographs and the captions in your group.

- Who would you like to meet? Why would you like to meet that person?
- What challenges do you think Marley and Kelvin are facing?
- How do you think they are trying to solve these challenges?

You will read more about Marley and Kelvin later.

In this unit, you are going to be talking about the future. You will be giving your own opinions about what other young people are doing, and what you would like to do. Let's start now.

To talk about the future, you add 'will' to the main verb. For example:

> I will study to be a teacher.
>
> They will work together on the project.

If you want to talk about something that happens in the future, that will continue to happen for a while, you use the future continuous tense.

It is formed by using will be + present participle, for example:

> He will be studying in London for three years.
>
> They will be working on a project in Bali.

PRACTISE

1 In your group, take turns to speak about your plans for the future. Use the mind map to help you. Add your own ideas too.

2 Now, respond to the other members of the group. Give your opinion of what others want to do. Here are some useful phrases for you.

- I like that idea because ...
- That is very interesting because ...
- I could never do that because ...
- I don't like that because ...

Try this

Write a short paragraph about your plans for the future. Use the mind map to help you. Give your paragraph to a friend. Check each other's spelling and grammar. Then, write a neat copy in your notebook.

Speaking and listening

Making a difference

1 Have you ever seen a beach that looks like the one in the photograph? Discuss this in your group.
- a What do you think should be done about it?
- b How would you go about solving this problem?
- c Who would you need to support you?
- d What kind of support would you need?

HINT

Here are some useful words and phrases to use when expressing your opinion.
- I think ...
- In my opinion ...
- I believe ...
- I feel ...
- My view is ...
- I don't think that ...

2 Listen to Audio 1.1, an interview with Melati Wisjen, from Bali. She and her sister, Isabel, decided to take action to solve a problem just like the one in the picture.

As you listen, think about these questions:
- a How did they get the idea for the protest?
- b Who did they get to support them?
- c What kind of protest tools did they use?
- d What do you think happened next?

DID YOU KNOW?

Protest tools that activists have used in the past include:
- marches
- food strikes
- interviews with the press
- workshops
- letters to influential people
- demonstrations
- **petitions**
- stay-aways.

DID YOU KNOW?

Bali is part of the island nation of Indonesia. Ocean currents have been carrying plastic pollution to the island of Bali for many years. Bali is a beautiful island, which relies on tourism for income. No tourists want to lie on the beach next to piles of plastic rubbish, so they really did need to find a solution!

▲ Melati and Isabel Wisjen, from Bali, Indonesia, started Bye Bye Plastic Bags

Do you remember?

To form the past tense, you add -ed to the main verb. For example:

I worked on my project.

They decided to do something about pollution.

There are exceptions, for example 'go' becomes 'went', 'speak' becomes 'spoke'.

PRACTISE

Revise what you know about tenses.

1 Put the verbs in brackets into the past tense.

What happened next, you might ask? Pastika (sign) a Memorandum of Understanding with the girls to work towards eliminating plastic on the island. The sisters (go) on to spread their message around the world. They (appear) on a TED talk, and (speak) at the UN. They also (participate) at the IMF World Bank Forum in Bali.

In 2019, the new governor of Bali (announce) a law banning single-use plastics, thanks to the sisters' efforts and to those of other non-profit organisations.

2 Now, put the verbs in brackets into the future tense.

Bye Bye Plastic Bags (grow). They now have 28 branches around the world. There (be) more branches soon. The whole movement (be) led by young people. As Melati Wisjen says, 'Bye Bye Plastic Bags (be) a platform where kids (feel) like their voices (be) heard.'

Try this

Melati Wisjen said: 'You see, we didn't want to wait until we were older to start making a difference ... It was more like, what can we do, as kids, right now?'

Think about a problem in your community that you could solve.

- What could you do to make a difference right now?
- What protest tools could you use?
- Whose support will you need?
- Is there someone you could write to, who would help you?

CHALLENGE YOURSELF

Prepare a short talk to give to the class about what the problem is, how you could solve it and who you would need to ask for support.

Speaking and listening

Listen to the sound of success

1 This is a photograph of Kelvin Doe, who built his own generator from scraps he collected in the garbage heaps in Sierra Leone. Listen to this **podcast** about his life in Audio 1.2.

2 Working in pairs, make short notes of the main points about Kelvin's achievements. Your teacher will play Audio 1.2 several times. Use this frame, and the phrases in the box below, to help you.

▲ Kelvin Doe, who built a generator from scrap materials found on garbage heaps

At 11 years old, ...

At 13, he made ...

Then, he built a ...

At 15, ...

Since then, he has ...

And now, he is ...

studying   built a generator   finding scrap electronics   made a battery
went to MIT   gave talks on a well-known show

HINT
You can do an internet search for Kelvin Doe's name to find out more about him, his inventions, his role as DJ Focus and the work he is doing now.

PRACTISE

1 Listen to Audio 1.2 again. Look out for the words in the list below.

2 Say these words out loud in your pairs. Note where the syllable breaks are, and where the emphasis falls in each word.

vi/ol/ent	ne/ces/si/ties	en/gin/eers	hon/or/ar/y
shor/tages	el/ec/tro/nics	in/ven/tion	po/ver/ty

3 Talk about Kelvin and his inventions. Use each of the words in a sentence, to show you understand its meaning.

4 Learn to spell the words.

Use of English

Working towards the future

The present perfect continuous tense is a verb tense that shows that an action has started in the past, and is still continuing in the present. It uses the has/have been + ing form of the verb. For example:

> Kelvin has been working with Emergency USA.
>
> They have been providing medical care to local people.

This tense emphasises duration – that a certain amount of time has taken place.

PRACTISE

1 Put the verbs in brackets into the present perfect continuous tense.
   - a Kelvin (collect) scraps from the garbage heaps for years.
   - b He (work) on a new design for a generator.
   - c His family (help) him to achieve his dreams.
   - d I (think) about studying engineering in the future.
   - e We (try) to start a recycling organisation for a while.
   - f You (want) to study at MIT for years, haven't you?

2 Change these sentences to questions, by changing the word order.
   - a He has been working on the plan for days.
   - b They have been looking for a solution for ages.
   - c She has been studying chemistry for four years.
   - d They have been working on an answer to the question.
   - e You have been building this since last week.
   - f She has been finding it difficult.

3 Make these statements negative, by adding 'not'.
   - a I have been reading about young activists.
   - b We have been collecting rubbish from the beach.
   - c They have been working until late at night.
   - d People have been donating towards the project.
   - e He has been studying in the USA.
   - f We have been spending money on research.

HINT

To ask a question, you change the word order. For example:

> Has Kelvin been collecting scraps for years?

HINT

To make a statement negative, you add the word 'not'. For example:

> She has not been studying this week.

You can abbreviate 'has not' to 'hasn't', and 'have not' to 'haven't'.

Reading

Read about a water crisis

1 Have you and your family always had access to clean drinking water? Talk about this in pairs.
   a Have you experienced a drought? What did you have to do to save water?
   b Have you ever turned on the tap and no water came out? What did you do?
   c How would you have to change the way you and your family live, if you had to fetch water every day, for drinking, cleaning and washing?

2 Read about how even a very young activist can make a difference. As you read the background to this story and the letters, think about these questions.
   a What action did Mari take to protest about the water supply?
   b What was it about her letter, in your opinion, that made the president reply to her?
   c How do you know the letter was written by Mari?

▲ The water supply in Flint was contaminated

Background

In 2016, the town of Flint, in Michigan in the USA, had been without clean water for over four years. People could not drink the water coming out of the taps, as it had been polluted by poisonous lead in the old water pipes. No one would take responsibility for fixing the problem; instead businesses and government were blaming each other.

People had to use bottled water for drinking, cooking and cleaning. Mari Copeny was going to Washington with her parents to take part in a protest about the Flint Water Crisis, but before she went, she decided to write a letter to President Obama. She was only 8 years old at that time so her letter does contain some spelling and grammar errors.

▲ Mari Copeny, also known as 'Little Miss Flint'

Amariyanna Copeny
Flint, Michigan

Submitted via whitehouse.gov
3/14/2016 6:02 PM

Mr. President,

Hello my name is Mari Copeny and I'm 8 years old, I live in Flint,Michigan and I'm more commonly known around town as "Little Miss Flint". I am one of the children that is effected by this water and I've been doing my best to march in protest and to speak out for all the kids that live here in Flint. This Thursday I will be riding a bus to Washington DC to watch the congressional hearings of our Governor Rick Snyder. I know this is pry a odd request but I would love for a chance to meet you or your wife. My mom said chances are you will be to busy with more important things but there is a lot of people coming on these buses and even just a meeting from you or your wife would really lift peoples spirits. Thank you for all that do for our country. I look forward to being able to come to Washington and to be able to see Gov. Snyder in person and to be ale to be in the city where you live.

Thank You
Mari Copeny

▲ Mari Copeny's letter to President Obama

THE WHITE HOUSE
WASHINGTON

April 25, 2016

Amariyanna Copeny
Flint, Michigan

Dear Mari:

Thank you for writing to me. You're right that Presidents are often busy, but the truth is, in America, there is no more important title than citizen. And I am so proud of you for using your voice to speak out on behalf of the children of Flint.

That's why I want you to be the first to know that I'm coming to visit Flint on May 4th. I want to make sure people like you and your family are receiving the help you need and deserve. Like you, I'll use my voice to call for change and help lift up your community.

Letters from kids like you are what make me so optimistic for the future. I hope to meet you next week, "Little Miss Flint."

Sincerely,

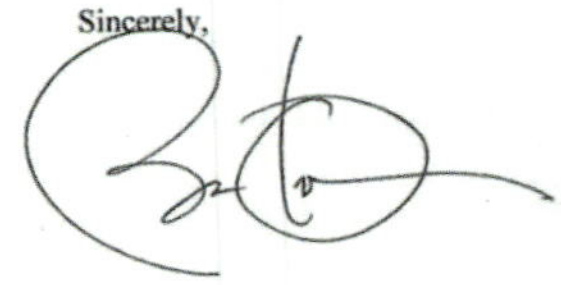

▲ Barack Obama's reply to Mari's letter

Vocabulary and spelling

Some words can be used as nouns or as verbs. There are quite a few of them in the reading texts. For example:

Don't bottle up your feelings. (verb)

I drank a bottle of water. (noun)

Do you remember?

Some words look similar, and are often confused. For example, you can travel by plane, over a big grassy plain, or you can meet at a restaurant, to eat meat.

Some words sound the same and are spelled the same, but have very different meanings! These are called homonyms.

Try this

1 Work in pairs. Write down sentences which show the meaning of each of the words in the box as
   a a noun
   b a verb.

trust	protest	chance	watch	march	raise	hope

2 Choose the correct words from those in brackets.
   a Mari was one of the children (affected/effected) by the water crisis.
   b She thought, 'I have nothing to (lose/loose) if I write to Mr Obama.'
   c She was (quite/quiet) determined to get him to visit Flint.
   d They did not need to (borrow/lend) money for the bus trip.
   e (Were/We're) very pleased that he came to visit.

3 Write sentences with these homonyms to show you know the two different meanings of each of the words.
   a dear
   b minute
   c hold
   d peer
   e press
   f trip

CHALLENGE YOURSELF

1 Put the sentences of this speech in to the correct order.
   a Next, I will make three promises to you, and you can hold me to them.
   b First, let me thank you for inviting me here today to listen to you, and to discuss the problem.
   c Secondly, or number two, rather, I will meet with the council this week.
   d Number three, I will have an answer on the water problem by the end of this week.
   e Finally, thank you all for your patience and kindness.
   f One, I will give this matter my utmost attention.

2 Now practise saying the speech aloud to your friend. Speak slowly and clearly, and remember to pause where there are commas and stop briefly for a breath at each full stop.

Use of English

The passive voice in the future

Sometimes you don't want to say who the person is doing an action, or you don't need to say who is doing an action, because everyone knows. This is when we use the passive voice.

The passive voice is very useful when you don't need to say who the 'doer' of the action is. For example:

Water pipes will be replaced.

People will be transported to the conference.

You can see that in both these examples, we know who has to replace the pipes (the government) and who will transport people to the conference (the organisers of the conference).

PRACTISE

1 Identify the passive voice in these sentences. Write the verbs in your notebook.
   - a We will be transported by bus.
   - b Refreshments will be served.
   - c We will be accommodated at the university.
   - d A new leader for Flint will be chosen by vote.
   - e The new pipes will be installed when we return.

2 Put the sentences below into the passive voice by
   - removing the 'doer'
   - changing the verb to will be + (verb)-ed.

   For example:

   The government will provide new pipes for the town Flint.

   New pipes will be provided for the town Flint.

   - a People will drink bottled water until then.
   - b The president will help the citizens of Flint.
   - c Mari will write a letter to the president.
   - d Police will assist with the crowds.
   - e The government will give bottled water to those in need.
   - f The city council will develop a new water system.
   - g The lawyers will win the case in court.
   - h The people of the city will elect a new mayor.

HINT
With the passive voice, the word order changes, and the object of the sentence becomes the subject. That's because the original subject, or the 'doer' in the sentence, has been removed.

HINT
Remember, some verbs are irregular, for example 'drink' becomes 'drunk'.

Future tenses

Do you remember?

In the first lesson, you learned about the future tense and the future continuous tense.

Future tense:

He will speak to the governor about the water problem.

Future continuous:

They will be installing the pipes next week. (the action continues for a while)

PRACTISE

Choose the correct form of the verb in brackets.

1 Marley (will study/will be studying) to be a teacher.
2 Kelvin (will spend/will be spending) time in Canada for the next few years.
3 He (will not stop/will not be stopping) lecturing at MIT.
4 The Wisjen sisters (will clean/will be cleaning) the beaches for a long time still!
5 They (will hold/will be holding) another Ocean Clean Up soon.
6 In the next lesson, you (will read/will be reading) about Marley Dias.

CHALLENGE YOURSELF

Write a letter to yourself in ten years' time. What will the world look like then? Tell your future self what you think you will be doing, and how you think the world will be organised then.

You do not have to show the letter to anyone. Seal it in an envelope and put it in a safe place. Write on the outside: 'To me in 20_____. Not to be opened until then!'

In ten years' time, hopefully you will find and open this envelope, and see if your hopes and predictions for the future came true.

Try this

Talk about you dreams for the future with a partner. Look at this photograph. Where does the path lead for you? What are your dreams?

Now write another paragraph, to follow the one you wrote in the first lesson. This time, look further ahead. Here are some questions to help you.

- Where will you choose to live?
- What will your dream job be?
- Where will you work?
- Will you have a family?
- What other dreams do you have?

Reading

Read a newspaper article

Marley Dias was often being told to read books about 'a white boy and his dog' at school. She wanted to read books about people who were more like her.

1 Work with a partner to talk about these questions:
   - a What books do you read at school?
   - b What types of main characters are usually in these books?
   - c Where do the stories usually take place?
   - d Do the books have a moral or lesson for the reader?
   - e Why did Marley decide to try and vary the books learners have access to in schools?

2 You are going to read a newspaper article about Marley and her mission. First, learn some new words, to help you understand the reading. Match the words on the left to their meanings on the right.

main character	Many different things
classic	An older, well-respected book
campaign	The main person in the story
variety	A book a person writes about their own life
autobiography	A plan to achieve a goal

3 Read the extract opposite from an article in *The Guardian* newspaper, written by Coco Khan.
   As you read, consider the following and make notes in your notebook.
   - a Who decides what students read at school?
   - b How do you think reading **affects** the way you think, and how you see other people?

4 Work with your partner. Quickly discuss, then write down, what you think the four main points are in this article. Use this mind map to guide you.

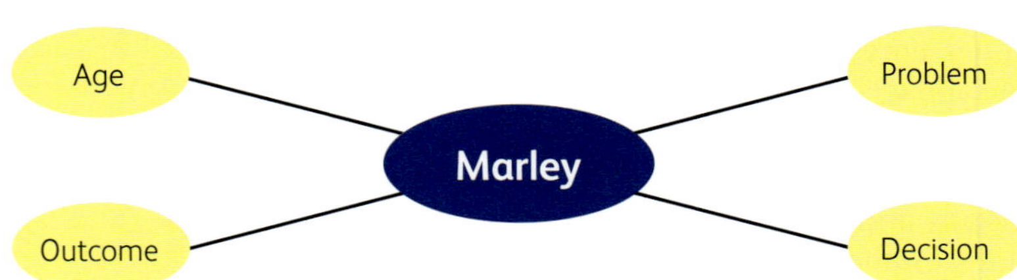

'They just wanted us to read about a white boy and his dog': why teenager Marley Dias fought back

She was 10 when she first decided to distribute children's books with black girl leads – a campaign that has taken her to the White House. Now she's written a book of her own.

By Coco Khan (adapted)

When Marley was 10 years old, she came home from school one day to eat pancakes with her mother and moan about having to read Where the Red Fern Grows by Wilson Rawls. Again.

'It's one of those "classic books" that's been in our school systems for so long! My great-grandparents remember when that book came out. I read it last year. And now I have to read it again this year. Every single year they want us to read a book about a white boy and his dog!'

Dias decided – at 10 years old – that she wanted to find and collect books that had black girls as the main characters in the story. Surely kids should read about a whole variety of different people? She wanted people to become aware of how many books there are with white boys as the main characters. She decided that she had to find 1000 books, featuring black girls. She was going to collect them and then donate them to the school her mother had gone to in Jamaica.

She created a hashtag, #1000BlackGirlBooks. 'Two of the first books I collected were Grace for President by Kelly DiPucchio and Brown Girl Dreaming by Jacqueline Woodson,' she says. She was looking for stories in which black girls 'can identify themselves and learn about their history' as well as 'open up to people who are different, to understand and to see and grow from those things we don't understand.'

Marley has become quite famous. Since she started the #1000BlackGirlBooks campaign in 2016, she has collected over 12,000 books. She has met some very well-known people – like Oprah Winfrey, and Ellen DeGeneres. She's also held a reading party at The White House! She's done all this while keeping up with her classes and doing her homework. What is that like for her? 'I don't really bring it up at school. Although I'm sure the kids at school know because they follow me on Instagram.'

'One author that I love is Tomi Adeyemi; she wrote Children of Blood and Bone, an African fantasy story. We don't often see black people in futuristic and magical worlds. For the black kids out there, who really love fantasy but never see themselves, they now feel a whole new level of connection. That's important.'

5 Answer these questions in your notebook.

a What irritated Marley about the books she and her classmates read in school?

b How many books was she trying to collect?

c Why did she send the books she collected to Jamaica?

d Name three books, mentioned in the article, that Marley loves.

e Write down two things that Marley has done that you admire.

f How do her classmates at school feel about her fame?

g What is your favourite book, and who is the main character?

DID YOU KNOW?

Marley Dias has written a book for teenage activists called *Marley Dias Gets It Done*. Perhaps your school can order a copy for the school library.

Speaking and listening

Listen to an innovative solution to litter

1 Have you heard about the Great Pacific Garbage Patch? Do some research on 'the Great Pacific Garbage Patch' in your group. You can look on the internet, or your teacher will provide you with reading material.
Find answers to these questions.
- a How big is the Great Pacific Ocean Garbage Patch?
- b Where is it?
- c What does it consist of?
- d Why is the Great Pacific Garbage Patch dangerous to sea creatures?
- e How is it dangerous to humans too?

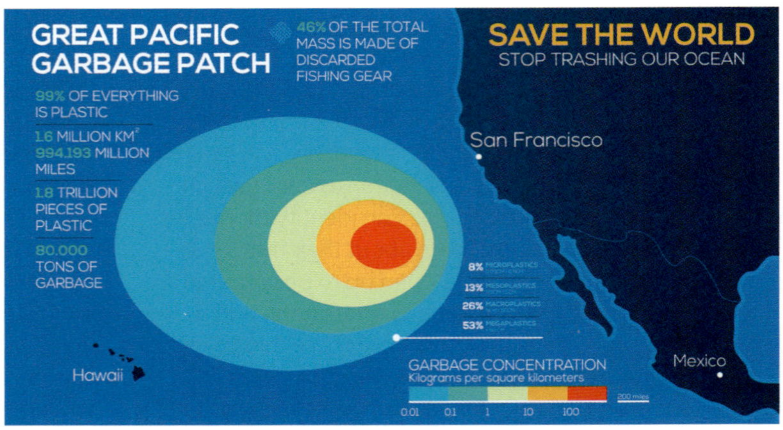

2 Listen to Audio 1.3, a true story about how a young inventor designed a device to help get rid of the problem of plastic in the ocean. Meet Boyan Slat, from the Netherlands.

▲ Boyan Slat invented The Interceptor

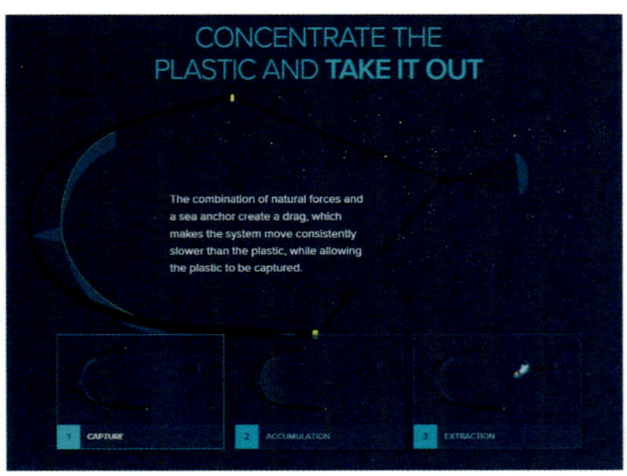

◀ The Ocean Cleanup website, demonstrating how the Interceptor works at sea

▶ The Interceptor, designed by Boyan Slat, in the harbour, ready for action

Try this

Answer these multiple-choice questions with a partner.

1 Boyan Slat invented
   - a The Interloper
   - b The Intermission
   - c The Interceptor.

2 It consists of
   - a a V-shaped screen into which the rubbish is funnelled
   - b a U-shaped screen and a floater, which collects even very small pieces of plastic
   - c a trapping screen which drifts on the ocean currents.

3 A **gyre** is
   - a a spiral pattern in the ocean currents
   - b a natural system of ropes and pulleys
   - c the way the screen is structured.

4 Slat's system works better than others because
   - a it follows the natural movement of the ocean
   - b it is powered by an engine
   - c it moves very quickly.

5 Once collected
   - a the trash is burned on board the ship
   - b the trash is transported to land to be recycled
   - c the trash is compacted into blocks.

6 The first Interceptor will be put to work
   - a in the Netherlands
   - b in San Francisco
   - c in the Great Pacific Garbage Patch.

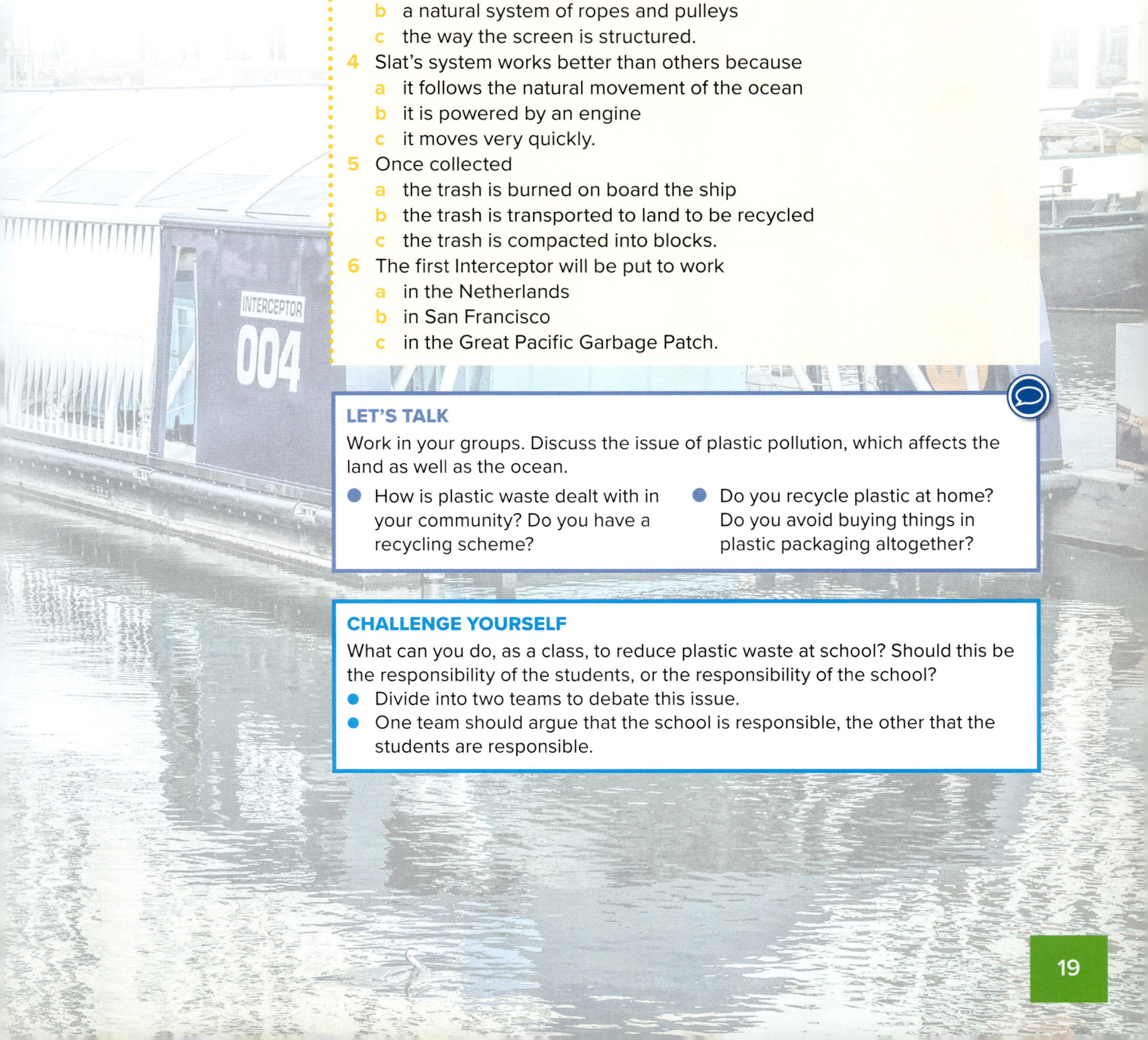

LET'S TALK

Work in your groups. Discuss the issue of plastic pollution, which affects the land as well as the ocean.

- How is plastic waste dealt with in your community? Do you have a recycling scheme?
- Do you recycle plastic at home? Do you avoid buying things in plastic packaging altogether?

CHALLENGE YOURSELF

What can you do, as a class, to reduce plastic waste at school? Should this be the responsibility of the students, or the responsibility of the school?

- Divide into two teams to debate this issue.
- One team should argue that the school is responsible, the other that the students are responsible.

Writing

▲ Can you show people a new way of looking at the world?

▲ Can you open someone's eyes to the possibilities around them?

Write a letter to a champion

You have read about, talked about and listened to, a variety of young activists who are making the world a better place. What can you do to improve the circumstances of something in your community?

In an earlier lesson, you spoke to the class about what you would do. Use your notes from that 'Challenge yourself' talk on page 9, to form the basis of a letter.

- Think about who can help you to achieve your goal – a well-known person, a politician, a celebrity.
- Write a **draft** letter to that person, asking them to help you to achieve your goal.
- Then ask a partner to check your letter for grammar and spelling mistakes.
- Use the format that you already know for a formal letter.

Do you remember?

How to write a formal letter

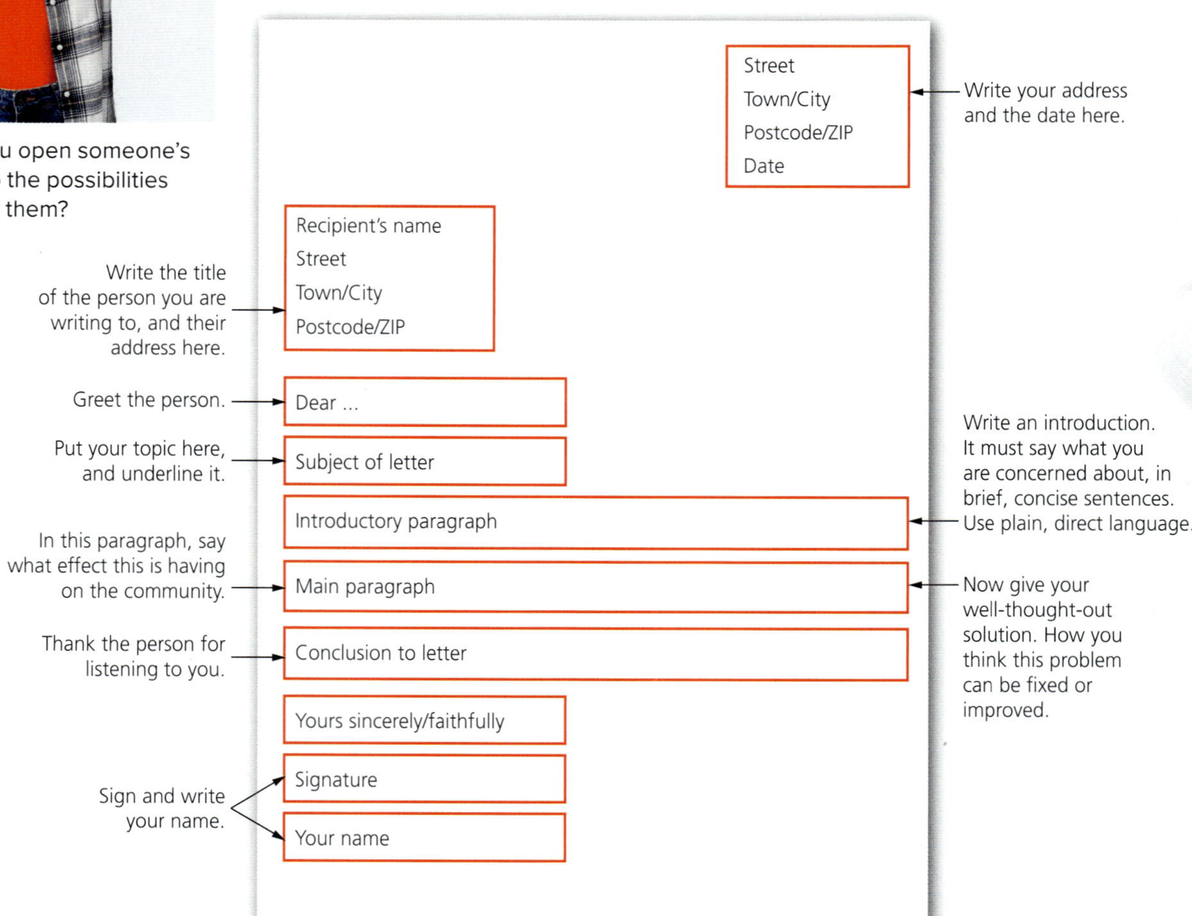

HINT

Remember to use formal language for a formal letter. For example, in your introduction, use phrases like:

I am concerned about ...

I wish to draw your attention to ...

The problem we have experienced in our community is ...

Thank you for taking time to read this letter.

Self check

Check that you:

- use the appropriate language for a formal letter
- use the correct format for a formal letter
- get someone to check your spelling and grammar before you write out a clean copy
- share your passion to improve something
- inspire someone to help you to achieve your goal.

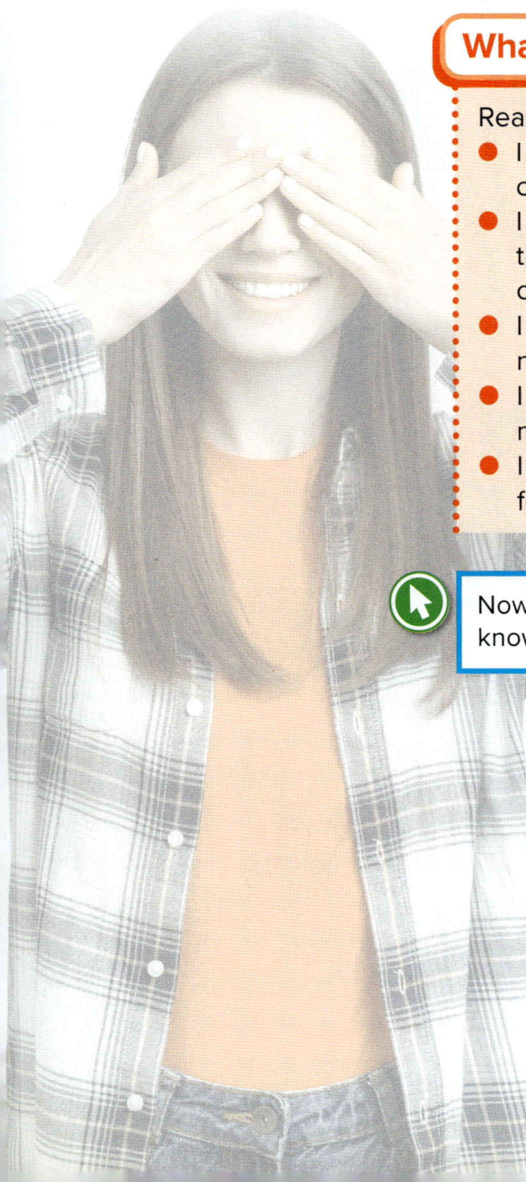

What can you do?

Read and review what you can do.

- I can listen to young activists talk about providing electricity for their community, and getting rid of plastic waste.
- I can give my opinion about young activists who are trying to change the world, and come up with my own solutions for a problem my community faces.
- I can read letters about a protest that a president got involved in, and a newspaper article about providing relevant books for black girls.
- I can write a letter to a well-known person asking for support for my campaign.
- I can use a range of future active and passive forms, future continuous forms and present perfect continuous forms.

Now you have completed Unit 1, you may like to try the Unit 1 online knowledge test if you are using the Boost eBook.

2 Travelling the world

In this unit you will:

- listen to friends talking about a holiday, to a fact and opinion interview about **eco-tourism** versus **over-tourism** and to a personal anecdote about eco-tourism
- talk about the benefits of tourism versus the harm that over-tourism can do; learn to recognise and separate fact from opinion
- read an article about an eco-lodge in the Jordanian desert, and a first-person account in a **blog** about a visit to the Lost City
- write a brochure advertising a tourist spot
- use the passive voice, abstract nouns, compound nouns and noun phrases, and a range of past modal forms.

◀ Some people want to explore unknown places

▲ Tourists queue to see the Acropolis in Athens

Speaking and listening

Travelling as a tourist

Have you and your family been away on holiday together? Talk about this in your groups.

- Where did you go? Was it a popular tourist destination?
- Were there many other tourists? Did you like that or not?
- Where would you like to go on holiday, if you had a choice?

Listen to Audio 2.1, of James telling Emily about his holiday. Choose the correct answer to these questions.

1 James did not enjoy his holiday because
 a he does not like croissants
 b he was in a bad mood
 c he had to visit too many museums and cathedrals with his parents.
2 Emily likes Paris because
 a she loves all the tourists in the museums
 b she loves the old streets and the food
 c she loves the 'Mona Lisa'.
3 James did not like the Eiffel Tower because
 a he had to queue for three hours to climb up it
 b it was rusty and pointy
 c it has a view.

▲ The Eiffel Tower has several million visitors a year

Try this

Look at the photographs. Read the captions out loud to a partner. Then discuss the statements and questions below.

1 Over-tourism happens when too many tourists visit a place. The tourists overuse the local resources because there are simply too many of them! You could say it is tourism that considers only the privilege of the tourist, and is not a partnership between the traveller and the people in the destination being visited.
 a What do you think it is like living in Paris? Imagine going to the supermarket, and getting to and from school.
 b What tourist hotspots are there in your country?
 c Have you visited any of them? What was your experience like?
2 Eco-tourism is defined as responsible, **sustainable** travel to natural areas, where travellers appreciate and respect the environment and wildlife. The tourism helps to support the local economy and involves local people. Often, there is an educational aspect to the trip.
 a What eco-tourism spots are there in your country?
 b Have you visited any of them? What was your experience like?

▲ Kerala, in India, is an unspoilt paradise, where eco-tourists are welcome

Speaking and listening

Listen to a radio interview

Listen to Professor Green discuss eco-tourism and sustainable tourism in the radio interview in Audio 2.2. As you listen, write answers to these questions in your notebook. Your teacher will play the audio twice for you.

1 Write down a definition for 'eco-tourism'.
2 Write down a definition for 'sustainable tourism'.
3 Why does Professor Green not like 'silly rich tourists' in Australia?
4 According to Professor Green, what makes eco-tourism successful?

Bias means that a person does not give equal chance to a certain idea, thing or group of people, or prefers an idea, thing or group of people over any other idea, thing or group of people.

You can be biased towards something. For example: I am biased towards books with a strong female character.

You can be biased against something. For example: My sister is biased against people who drive badly.

Try this

1 Discuss these questions in your group.
   a What things or events was James, in Audio 2.1, biased against?
   b What city was Emily biased towards in Audio 2.1?
   c What kinds of people is Professor Green, in Audio 2.2, biased against?
2 Work with a partner. Do you have any biases? Try to be as honest as possible.
   - Talk about what biases you may have towards certain ideas, people or places.
   - Talk about what biases you may have against certain ideas, people or places.

PRACTISE

1 See how many new words you can make with these roots and the prefixes and suffixes in the table.

over eco re	tourism respect use resource sustain	ful ly able

2 Work in pairs. Make sentences with the words you have made. Say your sentences to your partner.

Try this

Look at the photographs. Read the captions out loud to a partner. Then discuss the questions after below.

▲ It costs $1000 for a permit to go and see the lowland gorillas

1 In Rwanda's Parc des Volcans, tourists pay $1000 for a permit to visit the lowland gorillas. This makes several million dollars for the Rwandan government annually. The money is used to support the management and operation of Rwanda's protected areas.
   a How do Rwandans benefit from tourism?
   b How do you think Rwandans feel about tourists?
   c Do you think the fee for the permit is too much?
   d Does this fee show a bias towards certain people, in your opinion?

▲ The sea turtles of the Galapagos Islands

2 In 2007, the Galapagos Islands were on the 'in danger' list. Over-tourism was scaring away the sea turtles, who lay their eggs on the beaches. The islanders went all-out to change to a model of sustainable tourism.
   a What is the 'in danger' list?
   b Why do you think the islands were on this list?
   c What do you think the islanders did to protect the turtles? Think about the number of visitors, where the turtles lay their eggs and the fact that this happens at night.

CHALLENGE YOURSELF

Bring photographs of a holiday you have taken, or imagine taking, to class. Tell your classmates about your holiday. Be your own critic – was it a holiday to a tourism hotspot? How did you enjoy it?

Your classmates should ask you questions about your holiday, to:

- find out more about the details of your holiday, for example 'Where did you have dinner?'
- clear up anything that they didn't understand, for example 'How did you communicate, if you don't speak the same language?'

Use of English

Giving instructions using the passive voice

Do you remember?

In Unit 1, we learnt that we use the passive voice when we don't want to, or need to, say who the 'doer' in a sentence is. The passive voice is very useful when you want to tell people what to do, without saying who is going to enforce the rules!

Here's a quick reminder:

The tourism board charges a $1000 fee for a permit. (active voice)

A $1000 fee is charged for a permit. (passive voice)

PRACTISE

1 Read this Nature Park noticeboard.

2 Find all the examples of the use of the passive voice. Write them in your notebook. For example:

An entrance fee of $50 is charged.

HINT

When using the passive voice, the 'doer' of the sentence is removed. The object becomes the subject of the sentence and the verb changes.

In the present tense, the passive voice is formed by: is/are + ________-ed.

In the future tense, the passive voice is formed by: will be + ________-ed.

If there is still a 'doer' in the sentence, you will find the doer at the end, after the word 'by'.

For example:

A permit fee of $1000 will be charged by the tourism board.

Try this

Now, work in pairs to change each example of the passive voice into the active voice. For example:

The park charges a $50 entrance fee. Our guides speak Portuguese, English and Spanish.

Do you remember?

Modal verbs are helping words that are added to the main verb, to add extra expression.

So, for example, if you say 'We have to pay a fee', it is a definite statement.

If you say 'We might have to pay a fee', then there is some doubt or speculation.

What the modal verbs express	Modal verbs
obligation	must have
advice, opinion	should have
doubt, speculation	might have, may have
ability, deduction about past actions	can have, cannot have, can't have, could not have,could have, couldn't have

PRACTISE

1 Now use your knowledge of modal verbs to complete this set of instructions for visitors to Antarctica. Use modal verbs from the 'Do you remember?' box or your own choice of modal verbs.

Welcome to Antarctica!

You are about to embark on the adventure of a lifetime! Antarctica is fascinating, beautiful, freezing cold, and ___ be dangerous! We ___ ___ any accidents, so we ___ ___ a set of rules that everyone understands.

- Plans change. We ___ ___ wanted to visit the seals on a particular day, but the weather ___ ___ had a different idea, so we ___ have to spend the day cruising past icebergs instead. This is a once-in-a-lifetime journey! You ___ not see some of the things you wanted to, but there ___ be other, more interesting experiences in store for you!
- Dress appropriately. You ___ ___ cold weather gear. We ___ ___ anyone suffering from hypothermia.
- Your captain and his crew are in charge. They have years of experience, and if they ask you to do something, they ___ be obeyed, immediately. We ___ ___ people wondering off by themselves. Fog comes in quickly, and in the past there ___ ___ some tricky situations that ___ ___ become critical, if not for the fast response of the captain and crew.
- Finally, enjoy! Take time to experience what many people ___ ___ never seen in their lifetimes!

2 Write a postcard to a friend about what could have gone wrong, but did not. Your postcard should have at least five sentences on it. For example:

> Dear Marco,
>
> We had the most fantastic adventure, but it could have gone horribly wrong! We left our jackets on the plane. We would have frozen like ice cubes, but our guide lent us some old jackets. Otherwise we would have had to stay behind!
>
> From your ever-forgetful friend,
>
> Diego

CHALLENGE YOURSELF

At the end of this unit, you are going to write, edit and design a brochure for a place you would love to visit. Begin your preparations now.

- Decide on the place you will write the brochure about.
- Make notes about the kind of instructions you would need to give to visitors.
- Collect any tourist brochures that you can. There may be a travel agency nearby that could help you.

Keep your notes and add to them during the rest of the work in this unit.

Reading

Read about an eco-lodge in the desert

1 Work in pairs.
  a Which do you prefer – hot or cold?
  b Would you rather travel to Antarctica or to the Jordanian desert?
  c Talk about the brochure you are developing. What other ideas do you have? Discuss them with your partner. They may have useful ideas from a different perspective.

2 Read about the Fenyan Ecolodge in Jordan. As you read, **pay attention** to the text in inverted commas ('...'). Why do you think the writer used inverted commas in the text? These are some reasons you could consider:
- The writer wants to keep an authentic feel to the words.
- The text is a quote from another source, so you have to separate it from the writer's own words.
- The writer is separating her own opinion from the opinion she is quoting.
- The writer is remaining completely neutral.

The Fenyan Ecolodge is the first of its kind in Jordan. It was inspired by the caravanserai, which were roadside inns. These were places where traders and their caravans could rest and spend the night during their long journeys. These camel caravans followed the Silk Route, journeying across China, Central Asia and Europe, trading their wares and exchanging news as they went. They would stop at the inns along the way to rest and restock their supplies, before heading out on the next stage of their journey.

These inns were part of one of the first overland trading networks in the world, and they were places where travellers and pilgrims shared stories and knowledge, as well as buying and selling different goods.

It was this history that inspired the director of the Royal Society for the Conservation of Nature (RSCN) to call on the famous architect, Ammar Khammash, to build a modern version of a caravanserai.

The RSCN describes a caravanserai like this:

'A caravanserai is a building that looks square on the outside, with a single entrance, which is wide enough so that camels, and their loads, can enter. Inside, the courtyard is open to the sky. There are stalls along the inside walls for merchants and their servants, animals, and merchandise. The stone slabs in the front wall of the lodge are an old Yemeni way to control the temperature. They provide shade from the high sun during summer and absorb warmth from the winter sun to heat the building during the cool desert nights.'

They were lucky with the choice of the site. For once, conservation was more important than industry. The site the RSCN chose was along the western edge of the Dana Biosphere Reserve, and had been zoned for copper mining. Fortunately, the authorities decided that mining was not viable, and it would destroy one of the richest and most **diverse** wildlife areas in Jordan.

The Fenyan Ecolodge also employs local Bedouin people. Although the lodge is owned by the RSCN, it is run by EcoHotels, a Jordanian company. As their brochure says, 'Feynan Ecolodge cares about conservation and the community. We aim to have a minimal impact on the environment and offer a unique tourism experience. This is a 100% renewable energy hotel.' Feynan Ecolodge has won many awards, and has been listed as one of National Geographic's top 25 eco-lodges in the world.

Vocabulary and spelling

PRACTISE

1 Answer these questions.

- a Where did the caravans travel?
- b What was the purpose of their trips?
- c Why did they stop at caravanserai along the way?
- d What were the inns part of?
- e Why did the director of the RSCN call on a famous architect?
- f Why did the caravanserai have wide entrances?
- g What was the purpose of the big stone blocks?
- h What could have been built on the site, if the eco-lodge had not happened?

2 What do you think the writer's opinion of the Fenyan Ecolodge is? Read the text again and write down three phrases which show that she likes or dislikes the lodge.

3 Learn to spell these words about travel. If you do not know their meanings, look them up in your dictionary. Write down their meanings in your notebook.

caravan journey traveller pilgrim commerce accommodate merchant merchandise conservation diverse

CHALLENGE YOURSELF

- Draw a diagram of how you think a caravanserai would look when seen from above.
- Label your diagram, using information from the reading passage and the photograph.
- Share your drawing with your group. What is similar about your drawings? What is different? How did you interpret the photograph and the text, in comparison with the rest of your group?

Use of English

Noun phrases, compound nouns and abstract nouns

Try this

Describe this photograph using as many noun phrases, compound nouns and abstract nouns as you can. You can look at the text on the previous page for ideas too. For example:

The huge orange sand dunes gave me a feeling of peace.

↑ **noun phrase** (huge orange sand dunes) ↑ **abstract noun** (peace)

The heavily laden camels are on the pathway to the next town.

↑ **noun phrase** (heavily laden camels) ↑ **compound noun** (pathway)

Do you remember?

A noun phrase is a group of words (without a verb) that makes sense. For example:

The tall sand dunes in the desert are amazing.

Hundreds of people in large gas-guzzling tour buses are not really our target market.

If you are unsure whether a group of words is a noun phrase, see if it answers the questions 'who?' or 'what?' in connection with the verb. It helps to underline the verb in the sentence, to start.

PRACTISE

1 Write these sentences in your notebook.

2 Then, find the verbs in the sentences and underline them.

3 Finally, find the noun phrases and highlight them in a different colour or put a box around them.

a One definition of eco-tourism is responsible travel to natural areas.

b My sister is saving for the trip of a lifetime to the Amazon delta.

c Eco-tourism can provide work for people from the nearby communities.

d Many developing countries are interested in eco-tourism.

e Beautiful beaches and interesting ruins bring tourists to our country.

f Many tourists from all over the world can enjoy cruise trips around the islands.

Compound nouns are formed when two nouns are joined together. For example:

wild + life = wildlife

PRACTISE

1 Make compound nouns from the simple nouns in the trees. (Use one word from each tree in each compound noun you form.)

2 Use five of the compound nouns you have created in sentences of your own.

3 Identify the abstract noun in each of these sentences. Write them in your workbook.
- a In order to travel, she needs to get over her fear of flying.
- b I told her she just needs some confidence, and a good book to read on the plane.
- c She was in despair about this, so we decided to travel by train instead.
- d I respect her honesty though, it was a difficult decision to make.
- e They take great pride in the eco-lodge they have built.
- f Their hope for the future is that many tourists will come and visit.

4 Use an abstract noun from the 'Do you remember?' box, or your own choice of abstract noun, to complete each of these sentences.
- a They need to have ___________ in their ability to run the lodge.
- b What a huge ___________ it was! It is difficult to build in the jungle.
- c I've learned so much! For me ___________ only comes from trying to do things myself.
- d We wish you all ___________ in your new adventure.
- e Sometimes you have to rely on the ___________ of strangers when you are travelling.
- f We had so much ___________ travelling down the river on rafts!

Do you remember?

Abstract nouns are nouns that you can't see, feel or touch. Here are some examples.

fun kindness
love hope
fear joy
achievement
peace faith
glory wisdom
luck

Reading

A visit to the Lost City in Colombia

You are going to read part of a personal anecdote in this lesson, and then listen to the author describe the Lost City in the next lesson.

1 Work in pairs. Read this short introduction explaining what the Lost City is and where it is.
   a Find the location of the Lost City on a map.
   b Would you want to visit? Give your reasons, why or why not.
   c What does the writer of this factual piece imply about the trip? Find words that express his/her opinion.

The Lost City in Colombia

The Lost City, or Ciudad Perdida, is hidden deep in the jungles of Colombia. It was built in around 800CE, in the Sierra Nevada de Santa Marta mountains, by the Tairona people. This archaeological site only became an attraction after it was rediscovered in the 1970s.

You can't get there by boat, car or plane. The only way to access these ruins, buried in the jungle, is by a very tough five-day hike. There are several eco-friendly trekking tours for sustainable travellers, but you need strong legs and lungs to **reach** your destination in the tropical rainforest. This is probably very fortunate for the ruins, as it means only the very few, determined eco-travellers will visit.

▶ Trekking to the Lost City

2 Now read a traveller's blog, in which she tells us her personal experience of the Lost City.
   a As you read, make notes about her personal opinion of this trip.
   b Which words give you a clue that she is speaking about her own experience, as opposed to how other people may experience the trip?

Once in a lifetime

Colombia's 'Lost City' is older than Machu Picchu, and hardly anyone visits

Despite its challenges, I couldn't say no to an opportunity to visit Ciudad Perdida for myself.

▲ The Lost City, with its breath-taking terraces

The trek began in a small town called Mamey, a bumpy two-hour drive from the city of Santa Marta in the north part of the country along Colombia's Caribbean coast.

Visitors to the Lost City must be accompanied by a licensed guide, which can be easily booked online, through a handful of companies. Over lunch in Mamey, I got to know the 12 other hikers in my group and our guide Pedro.

The dirt path, which wove past large banana trees, towering palms and dangling vines, was challenging right from the start. It's recommended hikers have good general **fitness**, as the trek is difficult. On top of battling high temperatures and sweltering humidity, the 47-kilometre (29-mile) trek ascends and descends four small mountains – and because it's an out-and-back trail, we'd have to do it all twice. We shared the trail with mules, which carried food and other necessities to the various cabins where we would sleep along the way. The path snakes along the Rio Buritaca, which meant there were a few river crossings but also regular and much-welcomed chances to cool off …

The Wiwa people are descendants of the Tairona who have been left undisturbed for centuries. They have a deep spiritual connection with the land that continues today. Dressed in all white, a colour the Wiwa revere as holy, tribe members gave us a peek into their lives. They showed us how they strip the wax from palm leaves and use the fibre to make cross-body satchels called mochillas. They showed us their poporos, a device made from a gourd that holds powdered lime from seashells. … In the Wiwa community, a boy receives his poporo as a rite of passage into manhood.

The next morning, we began hiking in the pre-dawn hours, but high temperatures and muscle cramps had already set in by the time we reached the final stretch: 1,200 stone steps built by the Tairona. After finally lifting my sore body up the long flight of stairs, my eyes rested on the scene that had prompted the arduous journey: Ciudad Perdida.

3 Answer these questions in your notebook.

- **a** What does 'Ciudad Perdida' mean?
- **b** The writer mentions quite a few things she found difficult. Write down at least three of them.
- **c** How many people made up their party?
- **d** Draw and label the distance and the 'shape' of this journey.
- **e** Is the writer correct when she says the Wiwa people 'have been left undisturbed for centuries'? Explain your answer.
- **f** What is a poporo made of, and what is it used for?
- **g** Why is a boy given a poporo?
- **h** What was the final challenge the author faced?

Speaking and listening

Listen to the history of the Lost City

1 Work in a group. Talk about what you already know about the Lost City, from the previous lesson.

- How would you describe the journey there?
- How would you describe the Lost City, based on the traveller's blog and the photographs in this unit?

Listen as the author continues her description of the Lost City in Audio 2.3. As you listen, select the answers to these multiple-choice questions, and write them in your notebook.

2 The mountain slope consisted of
  a a set of wooden terraces carved into the mountainside
  b a series of stone terraces set into the hillside
  c a set of crests in the lush forest.

3 The group was quiet because
  a they were exhausted and respectful
  b Pedro was talking
  c they were resting their eyes.

4 The Lost City consists of
  a remote protected forests
  b 169 terraces built over 30 hectares
  c 30 terraces built over 169 hectares.

▲ The guide explains the rules to the eco-travellers

5 In 1972
   a explorers discovered treasure in the forest
   b traders followed the stone steps and found the City
   c looters uncovered gold, jewellery and ceramics.

6 '**Looting**' means
   a stealing things you should not
   b ignoring a problem
   c destroying the local environment.

7 What did the author marvel at, as she sat on one of the highest terraces?
   a That there were so few tourists
   b That she was a very lucky woman
   c That it was unlike any other tourist attraction.

8 What mental hurdle did she have to overcome at the end?
   a The big jump down the terraces.
   b Having to do the whole trip again in reverse to get back.
   c That she had accomplished her goal.

LET'S TALK

1 Work in a group. Sometimes people don't say exactly what they mean. Look at these two sentences from the audio extract. Discuss the sentences. What does the writer actually mean?
   a I couldn't say no to an opportunity to visit Ciudad Perdida for myself.
   b Earned views are always better.

2 Listen as your teacher plays Audio 2.3 again. Read through the reading text on page 33 again too.
In your group, write down five questions about this trip, that you would like answers to.
   - Practise asking the questions in your group.
   - Then take turns to ask another group your questions.
   - The other group then answers the questions.

Try this

Have you done a walk or a hike to a place of great beauty?
- Share your experiences.
- How did you feel when you reached your goal?

Writing

Write a tourist brochure

You are going to write a brochure about a place you would love to visit. You make a Z-fold brochure or use one A4 sheet of paper, like in this illustration.

Z-fold brochure

A4 brochure

Try this

Here are some pointers about the information you need to include. You do not have to use this order, but all this information needs to be your brochure.

- Factual information about the place, its features, how to get there, where to stay. This can be one paragraph or a bulleted list of information.
- If this is an eco-lodge/eco-adventure, then boast about it. Tell the reader about your sustainable energy or about how you support local communities.
- Your opinion – you are trying to sell this destination! Tell the reader how fantastic, amazing, incredible the place is. Include photographs, and perhaps a map if that is useful.
- Convince the reader that they have to go there. Support your argument with quotes from people who have had a wonderful time.
- Finally, a contact email or telephone number.

HINT

You can invent a totally imaginary place if you like, you don't have to use a real destination.

Self check

Use this checklist to make sure you have covered all the details needed in your brochure.

Planning and structure:

- mind map or diagram
- list of features of your destination – the facts
- opinion – why and how fantastic the destination is
- supporting evidence from satisfied visitors
- photographs.

Sentences:

- are properly constructed
- are punctuated correctly
- are varied (some questions, statements, exclamations, etc.).

Words:

- are spelled properly
- are right for this brochure – you are selling the destination!
- are interesting and/or informative.

Voice and style:

- is right for this kind of brochure/audience
- is light-hearted, but not too slangy.

CHALLENGE YOURSELF

Present your destination and your brochure to the class. Let the class vote for the top five brochures and destinations that they want to visit.

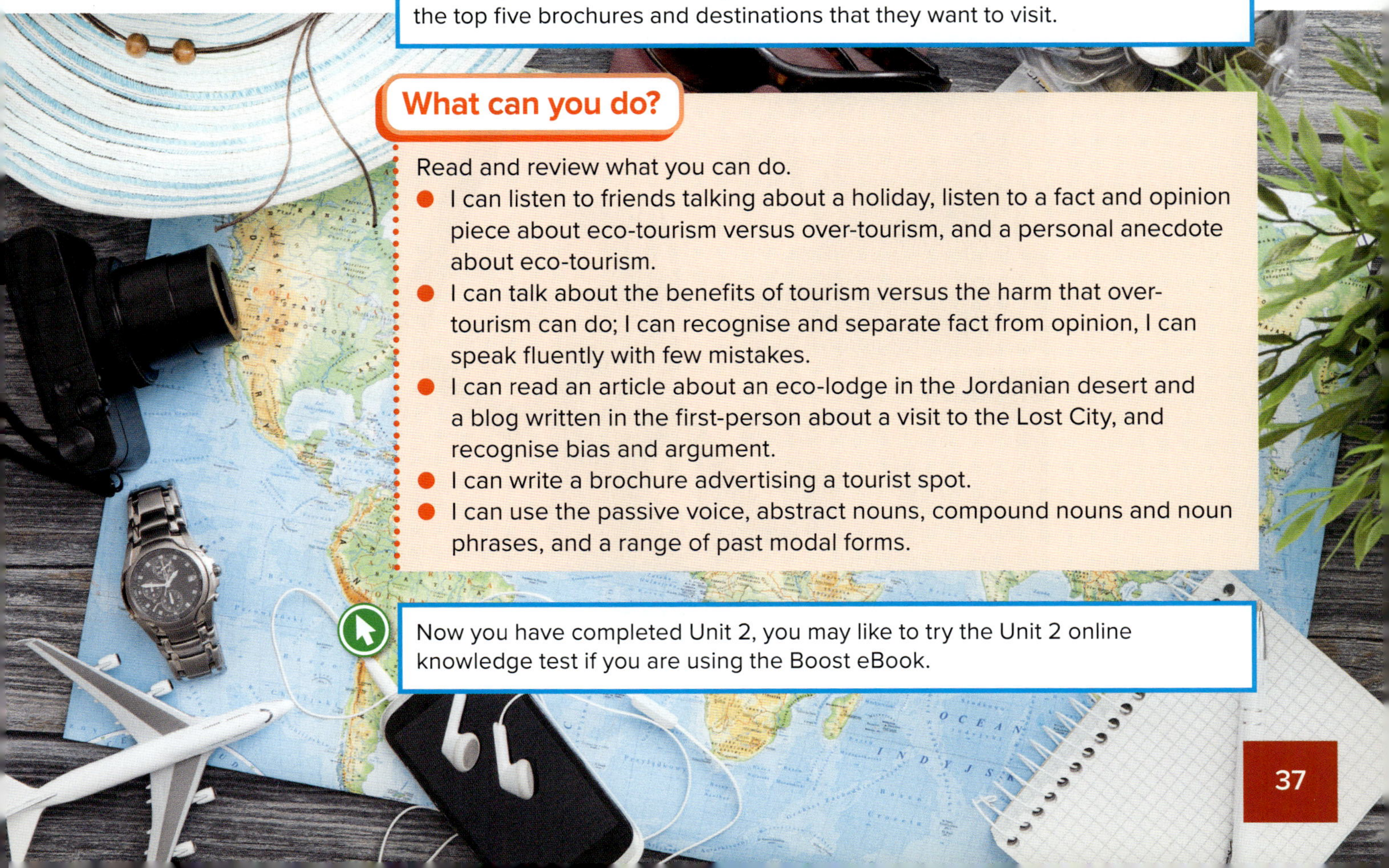

What can you do?

Read and review what you can do.

- I can listen to friends talking about a holiday, listen to a fact and opinion piece about eco-tourism versus over-tourism, and a personal anecdote about eco-tourism.
- I can talk about the benefits of tourism versus the harm that over-tourism can do; I can recognise and separate fact from opinion, I can speak fluently with few mistakes.
- I can read an article about an eco-lodge in the Jordanian desert and a blog written in the first-person about a visit to the Lost City, and recognise bias and argument.
- I can write a brochure advertising a tourist spot.
- I can use the passive voice, abstract nouns, compound nouns and noun phrases, and a range of past modal forms.

Now you have completed Unit 2, you may like to try the Unit 2 online knowledge test if you are using the Boost eBook.

3 Well-being

In this unit you will:

- listen to a physical **workout** podcast
- talk about healthy living and well-being
- read an article about mindfulness and teenage brains
- write an informal text to advise a friend on healthy living and well-being
- use different types of adjectives in different ways
- use a range of prepositional and phrasal verbs.

Speaking and listening

A healthy mind in a healthy body

You have probably heard people talk about a 'healthy mind in a healthy body'. The idea is that if you keep your body healthy (by exercising and eating well), then you will also have a healthy mind that allows you to study and work well.

So how do you keep your body healthy? Perhaps you have done a workout online, with a fitness coach.

1 Quickly tell your group about two things that you do to keep your body healthy.
2 You are going to listen to a podcast workout. Before you listen, match these words and diagrams.

run	jog	squat	reach up	crunch	plank	push up

3 Then, tell your group about other workout **exercises** and movements you may know (such as stretch, twist, touch toes, rotate, circle, etc.).
4 Now, listen to the podcast in Audio 3.1 carefully. Make a note of any instructions you do not understand. Ask others in the group for help if necessary.

HINT

Remember to use the imperative forms of verbs in your instructions. For example:

Touch your toes.
Now stretch up into the air.

Listen to the intonation in the instructions on the podcast and try to say yours in the same way.

PRACTISE

Find a space where you can exercise. Listen to the podcast again and do the exercises suggested as you listen.

Try this

In your groups, develop a short workout for your class to follow.

- Start with a short warm-up activity.
- Then provide five short and easy exercises.
- Remember, give clear instructions for each exercise.

Take turns in groups to provide the workout for your class. You can record your workout and play it back to the class, or you can give a 'live' class.

Speaking and listening

Listening for specific information

1 Listen to Audio 3.2, a podcast about Joe Wicks. As you listen, write down five facts about him. Remember that a fact is information that can be checked.

2 Listen again and check your facts. (For example, is the date correct? Is the name correct?)

DID YOU KNOW?

A fitness coach is a person who helps you to reach your health and fitness goals through an exercise plan designed especially for you. Most professional sportspeople have fitness coaches who help them develop and maintain fit and healthy lifestyles.

Try this

Work in pairs. Share the facts that you wrote down with your partner and discuss them until you agree on a summary of the main facts about Joe Wicks given in the podcast. Ask and answer questions like this:

Q: Is this important? He is known as 'The Body Coach'.

A: Yes, and we can check that fact online.

Q: What about this? He is widely recognised.

A: I don't think that is so important. Can we check it? Not really, but I see what you mean. He is famous, so I suppose that is a fact too.

PRACTISE

Make up a combined fact sheet about Joe Wicks. You can add other information about him as well. Display this in your classroom.

Try this

1 Read what the following three fitness coaches have to say about maintaining a healthy lifestyle. Take notes of the main ideas in each text.

A I am shocked when people say that exercise is boring. It does not need to be! In fact, the secret is to do different types of exercise. If you enjoy nature, run in the forest. If you like the beach, try doing your workout on the sand. If music gets you going, switch it on and enjoy your favourite songs while you exercise. Some people even exercise while cleaning up the house. Walk or cycle to the shops or to school instead of using public transport if you can. You can do twice as many steps in a day, just by doing simple things like this. And yes, track your steps on your phone or watch. Set a goal and see if you can reach it every day.

B Just because you exercise regularly doesn't mean that you can eat anything you like. A healthy lifestyle involves exercising and eating a balanced diet, including the best fresh food you can. If you want to improve your lifestyle, you should pay twice as much attention to the type of food that you eat. You could start by eating half as much cake and other sweet treats as you usually would – try fruit instead! You do not need expensive supplements, you need a balance of fresh and healthy meals which will give you proteins, vitamins, minerals, fats and carbohydrates. Oh, and don't forget the fresh, clean water. If your tap water is safe, drink that, otherwise boil and filter your water before you drink it. You don't need to buy plastic bottles of water.

C The aim of an exercise is to improve how your body works so it is all the more important that you learn to exercise correctly. Once you have done your warm up, start your exercise routine. Time yourself and be disciplined. If you need to do 20 repeats, do 20 repeats, not 15! Look in a mirror as you work out so that you can check you are doing the exercise correctly. This is the only way you will achieve the lifestyle that you wish for.

2 Work in groups and discuss each statement. Say whether you agree or disagree with each one, and why.

3 Develop your own set of tips about how to maintain a healthy lifestyle. You can include some of the ideas that you have discussed. Then think about how you can present your ideas to the rest of the class.

HINT

Your tips should be short, clear and to the point.

Choose your words well. The correct terminology and interesting words will make the class pay attention.

CHALLENGE YOURSELF

1 Look at the images here which show healthy minds at work. Then draw your own picture to show how you view the idea of a healthy mind in a healthy body. Your picture can be realistic or abstract.

2 Write a paragraph or a short poem about your picture.

Do you remember?

Compound adjectives are formed when two descriptive words are joined together by a hyphen. Often, participles make up the second half of the compound adjective.

Examples:

a well-recognised coach, a record-breaking podcast

HINT
Join compound adjectives with hyphens, for example well-respected.

If the adjective ends in -ing and is made from a verb that ends in -e, drop the -e. For example, bore becomes boring.

HINT
Adjectives that end in -ed describe feelings.

Adjectives that end in -ing describe characteristics.

Use of English

Adjectives are very useful!

Using a range of adjectives is one of the many ways you can improve the style of your writing.

We can use intensifying adjectives like 'absolute' or 'complete' to make the meaning stronger. For example:

She was an absolute star.

The performance was a complete success.

Their attempt was a total failure.

We can also use compound adjectives as intensifiers. For example:

She is a world-famous actor.

He was a hard-working student.

PRACTISE

Adjectives are very useful in descriptions and they can be used in many different ways. Can you spot all the adjectives in these paragraphs?

1 Joe Wicks is not only one of the most widely-recognised fitness coaches in the world, he is also a **particularly** successful author. His best-selling cookbook of healthy 15-minute meals, *Lean in 15*, has sold more than 900,000 copies. And that was his first book! It's a particularly fascinating success story. If I could be half as successful as him, I would be happy!

2 I start my fitness routine with a five-minute warm-up. This is extremely important as it prevents injuries. The astonishing thing is that many people don't do this. It's a **proven** way to begin your daily exercise routine.

Write the adjectives in your notebook and practise spelling them correctly.

Try this

Choose the best adjective to complete each sentence.

1 I am (shocked/shocking) by the number of people who do not warm up before they exercise.
2 That is a (bored/boring) exercise. Why don't you try something else?
3 She is a (highly respected/highly respecting) lifestyle coach.
4 They are such a (healthy-looked/healthy-looking) couple. I bet they work out every day.
5 I love doing press-ups. They are my (absolute/absolutely) favourite.

Try this

Do some research and write a paragraph about Joe Wicks or another famous fitness coach. Your paragraph should have six or seven sentences and you should use at least one adjective in each sentence.

Self check

- Try to use the different types of adjectives you have revised above.
- Check the spelling of the adjectives you use carefully.

CHALLENGE YOURSELF

1 Work in pairs and rewrite these sentences, replacing the underlined words in each sentence with compound adjectives.

a Many health blogs featured his cookbook that has sold the best. The coach has recipes for making meals in 15 minutes.

b Did you listen to that podcast that has broken all the records?

c She started out as a coach who worked part time, and now she is a coach who is famous all over the world.

2 Then, say each new sentence aloud with the compound adjective. You will have to change the word order in the sentences.

As you know, adjectives are also useful for making comparisons. For example:

He is a better coach than I am. Is he as good as Joe Wicks? He is the best coach in the country!

Look at how we can use the words 'half' and 'twice' and 'all the more' to make comparisons. For example:

Because the aim of exercise is to improve, it is all the more important that you learn to exercise correctly.

People should pay twice as much attention to the type of food that they eat.

If you eat half as much cake as you usually do, you should soon start feeling healthier.

PRACTISE

Work in pairs and complete these comparisons with the words from the box below. Check carefully to be sure each sentence makes sense. You can use the same words more than once.

1 Who do you think is the _______ fitness coach in our town?
2 I am much healthier because I eat _______ as I used to.
3 You need to drink _______ water as you usually do to keep hydrated.
4 Can you show me a _______ way to do this exercise? I keep hurting myself!
5 I am learning to dance, although I am not half _______ you are yet!
6 Exercising on the beach is _______t it gets. Fresh air and a beautiful environment too.

best	as good as	better	twice as much	half as much

Reading

Mindful or mind full?

Before you read the next article, you are going to do an activity which is designed to make you more **mindful**.

1 As you listen to Audio 3.3 and complete the activity, think about what it means to be mindful. Then have a quick discussion with your group about what you thought, what you heard and what you felt while you did the exercise.

2 Read these tips about things you can do to be more mindful. As you read, think about the things that you may already do to be more mindful.

Mindfulness

Most of us worry about all sorts of things all the time. *Why did a friend say that? Why didn't I get good marks in the test? What is wrong with my parents? Why did I get sick?* We tend to pay attention to what is wrong in our lives. Learning to be mindful can help us when we are down. It can also help us to calm down, relax and to pay attention to other things. This has many benefits, not the least of which is that it helps us to deal with the stress of everyday life. And less stress means better health!

Mindfulness is the state of being aware of the present moment. In this time, we focus on ourselves or on our bodies. We may think about how parts of our body feel or we may focus on the way we are breathing. When life gets tough, sometimes it is useful to stop and concentrate on being mindful. We can do simple exercises like the one you have already done to help create this state. But there are others things that we can do to become more mindful generally.

Some tips for developing mindfulness:

- Stop talking, and listen to others. The Dalai Lama once said 'When you talk, you are repeating what you already know. When you listen, you may learn something new.'
- Be kind, not cruel to others. Don't bully people or hurt them. And be kind to yourself too.
- Learn to **meditate**. Meditating can help you to stop and breathe and this helps you to deal with stressful situations.
- Focus on one thing at a time. Declutter your time and your life. This will help you avoid feeling overwhelmed or fed up with things.
- Accept that some things change in life and you cannot control everything. Focus on positive changes you can make in your own life to benefit yourself and others. Keep calm and carry on.

Try this

Work in groups. Discuss the text you have read. Answer these questions.
1 What does 'mindfulness' mean?
2 Give five examples of ways the writer says you can develop mindfulness.
3 Do you know any other ways of developing mindfulness?
4 What does the writer think about mindfulness? What does the author say that supports his or her opinion? (Hint: Read the first paragraph again.)

Vocabulary and spelling

1 Listen to Audio 3.4. Pay attention to the way the underlined words are pronounced in the sentences below. Then, in pairs, repeat the sentences.
- Take a deep breath. Now breathe out slowly.
- Mindfulness is the state of being aware of the present moment.
- Meditating can help you to deal with stressful situations.

2 Work in pairs. Say each pair of words. Then make a sentence with each word to show you understand the meaning and how to use it in a sentence. Make sure you can spell these words:
a breath (noun); breathe (verb)
b mindful (adjective); mindfulness (abstract noun)
c stress (noun), stress (verb); stressful (adjective)
d present (noun), present (verb).

HINT
Some words may have more than one meaning. Choose one meaning to feature in each of your sentences.

LET'S TALK

Our minds are always full of information – things to remember, things to do, deadlines, preparations for parties and exams, and so on. We often worry about negative things. We are always busy! But being mindful can help. How?

In your groups, have a quick discussion about the differences between having a **mind full** and being **mindful**. Answer the questions that follow to guide your discussion.

Having a full mind
- What do you think about when you wake up in the morning?
- What do you think about at school?
- What do you think about when you eat?
- What things worry you?

Being mindful
- What can you do to stop worrying about something?
- What can you do to have a quiet moment by yourself?
- Do you ever think about the way you breathe?
- Do you make time every day to think about the things in your life that make you happy, and things you are grateful for?

Share your group's ideas with the class. Your suggestions might be very helpful to someone else, even if they don't say so.

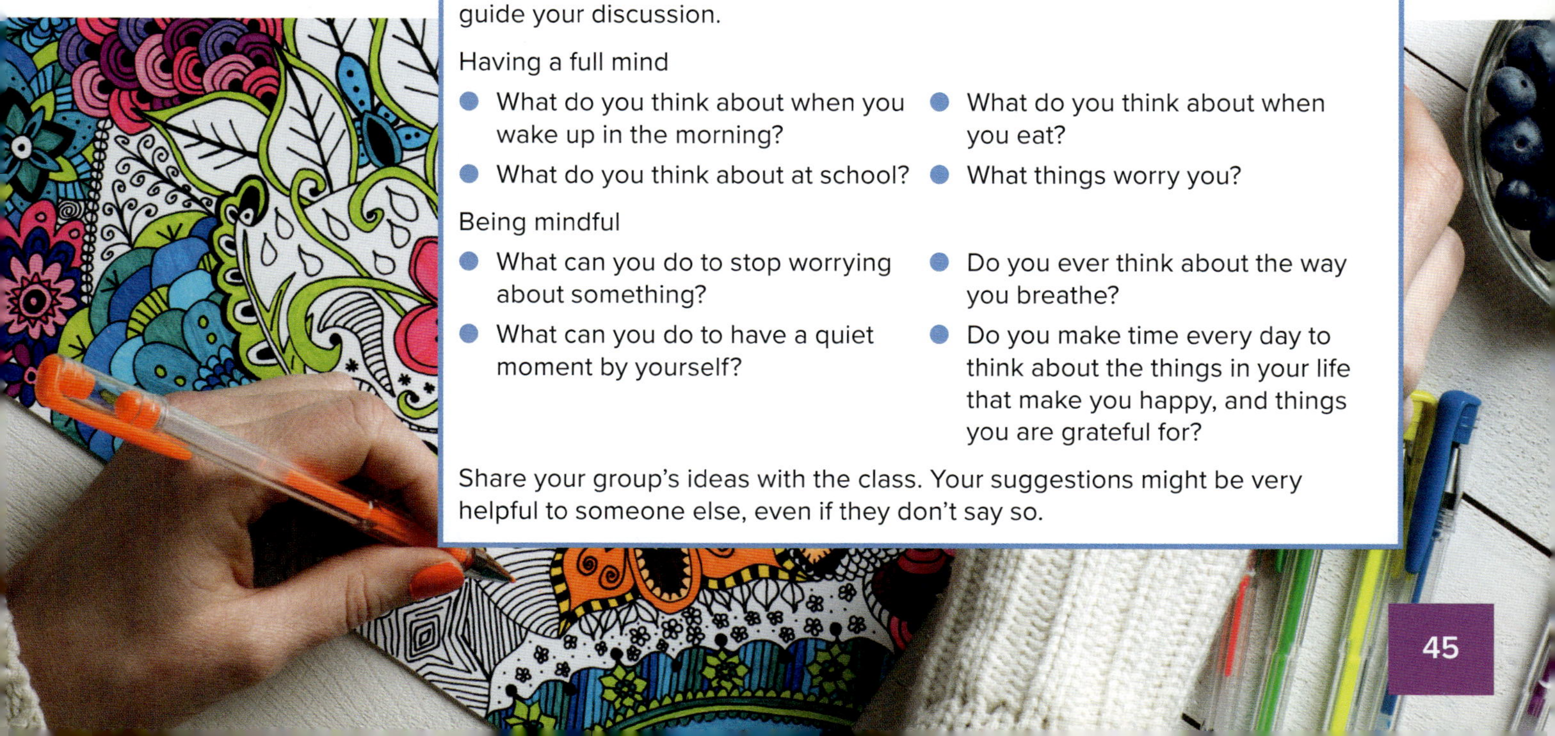

Use of English

Prepositions with verbs

PRACTISE

Choose the correct preposition to complete each of these sentences.

1 I learned (to/of) be more mindful and it really helps.
2 When things get tough, stop and concentrate (in/on) your breathing.
3 Don't think (on/about) what you read in the news yesterday.
4 My friends say I should pay attention (to/from) them.
5 Try to forget (from/about) the messages on your phone for 30 minutes every day.
6 Anna and Lee belong (to/in) a meditation group.

Do you remember?

We use verbs with certain prepositions. For example:

✓ I agree with you.

✗ I agree to you. I agree at you.

✓ She worries about exams and tests.

✗ She worries on exams and tests. She worries for exams and tests.

Note the order of the words in the sentences. We cannot put the preposition at the beginning of the sentence:

✗ With you I agree.

✗ About exams she worries.

Try this

1 Work in small groups. Listen to the conversation in Audio 3.5. Then use prepositions to complete the phrases in the short conversation below.

Lee: Do you know __________ mindfulness activities?

Pablo: Oh. You mean meditation? I don't really believe __________ that, but maybe it can help sometimes.

Anya: So, who or what do you turn __________ when you have a problem?

Mina: My sister helps __________ lots of things, so I usually turn __________her.

Anya: I belong __________ a mindfulness group. We meet and talk __________ this every week.

Lee: Can you tell me more __________ it?

Anya: Yes of course. If you promise to listen __________ me!

Pablo: He'll listen, but he won't agree __________ you.

Mina: You don't have to agree __________ everything you hear!

Do you remember?

Some expressions with verbs and prepositions are tricky to understand because the meaning is idiomatic. If you try to understand each word separately you may not be able to work out the real meaning of the phrase. These are called phrasal verbs.

2 Listen to the conversation again and take note of which word or words in each sentence are emphasised.
3 Practise the conversation in groups of four. Try to use the correct intonation when you do this.

DID YOU KNOW?

An idiom is a group of words with a special meaning. For example:

What do you do when you are down? (To 'be down' means to feel depressed or sad.)

Meditating helps me to calm down. (To 'calm down' means to relax.)

I just blow up when things get tough. (To 'blow up' means to get angry and lose your temper.)

Sometimes it is hard to work out what people really mean. (To 'work out' means to understand.)

PRACTISE

Work in pairs. Read these sentences and look at the underlined phrases. What do you think they mean? Choose the correct meaning from the box under each sentence. Then check in a dictionary to see if you are correct.

1 All my plans fell through last week and now I feel sad.

fell on the ground	didn't work out

2 Have you ever come across an exercise called 'yawn and stretch'?

heard about or seen	move from one place to another

3 Mara is planning to find out more about yoga as part of her mindfulness programme.

learn or discover	to see

4 We get together for mindfulness exercises before we begin the class.

get in a group	collect things

5 When life gets difficult, I try to keep calm and carry on.

lift up heavy things	continue to do what you are doing

6 Don't look down on students who do not wear designer shoes.

think you are better than	stare at from above

CHALLENGE YOURSELF

Use the following phases in sentences of your own:

- help out
- bump into
- burn out.

Give your sentences to a partner to read. Discuss the sentences and give each other feedback about how to improve them.

Reading

Teenage brains

1 Before you read this next opinion article:

a Work in small groups and discuss the risk-taking profile of your group.
- Do you take risks?
- Why do you take or not take risks?
- What do you gain from taking or not taking risks?

b Look at the photograph on the left. Do you see yourself as the cat sees itself? Is this how risk-takers see themselves?

c Report back to the class briefly.

DID YOU KNOW?
A person who takes risks is called a risk-taker. A risk-taker does things that involve some kind of danger.

HINT
Exurbia refers to the region outside the suburbs of a city.

2 Read the article below carefully and try to understand the opinion of the writer as you read. What does the author think about teenagers who take risks?

Teenage risk-taking – the positive side

Adolescence is the time between childhood and adulthood. It is a time when our bodies and minds grow up. Our bodies change shape and our brains also change and develop. Our brains become more efficient and the connections in our brains become stronger so that we can do more complex tasks. We become **mature**. This process takes many years.

There has been much debate about the age at which our brains are fully mature. At 25? Or at 16? In many countries, people are allowed to vote for the first time at the age of 18, or to join the army to fight, so presumably the governments think people are mature by the age of 18.

And yet 16-year-olds can be very successful entrepreneurs and **influencers**.

Steven Johnson, in an article for *The Washington Post* in March 2020, said the following about teenagers:

'They invent dances, **coin** slang, lead political movements, make Bookstagrams and draw millions of views to Minecraft and makeup streams. They learn second languages and sonatas. From crammed city apartments and the finished basements of exurbia, they generate colossal revenue on YouTube and iterate endlessly on TikTok, whose billion-plus users have helped make parent company ByteDance one of the world's most valuable start-ups.

Why don't teenagers get more credit?'

Scientists say that the last part of our brains to get properly connected are the parts at the front – the frontal and prefrontal cortices. These parts of our brains control what we do and the risks that we take in doing these things. This may explain why very smart young people can be **impulsive** and also why they may do things that seem stupid to older people. It may also explain why young people can be so creative.

Some older people look down on teenagers for being untidy or rude, or for taking silly risks. In the past, this has been explained by the idea that teenage brains are not fully developed. But perhaps there has been too much focus on the negative effects of this risk-taking and not enough focus on the really positive effects. We need to work out what these positive effects are. Taking risks can also help us to learn and create in a way that more mature brains perhaps cannot. Furthermore, there is some evidence that positive feedback from others may help teens to take risks successfully. So, maybe there should be more emphasis on the positive side of risk-taking and the benefits it can bring.

So, I would agree with the people who say that teenagers could and should be allowed to help to inject new energy and ideas into our world.

Vocabulary

1 Match these words and their definitions. Write each word alongside its correct definition in your notebook.

inject (verb)	The outer layer of the cerebellum in the brain
impulsive	To make up or invent a new phrase or expression
cortex (plural cortices)	Adult, grown-up
mature	Doing something without thinking about it first
adolescence	To introduce something new
coin (verb)	The time during which a young person becomes an adult

2 Use the correct forms of the words in the table above to complete these sentences.

- **a** We can rely on young people like Greta Thunberg to ____________ some new ideas into our lives.
- **b** Do you know who ____________ the expression 'I just want to be alone'?
- **c** I am not an ____________ person! I plan everything first.
- **d** Please show me where the frontal ____________ are on this model of a brain.
- **e** Pablo is only 16, but he is very ____________ for his age.
- **f** For many young people ____________ is a difficult time during which they feel misunderstood.

Read the opinion article again and choose the answer to each question below.

3 How do are our brains change during adolescence?
   a The connections between parts of the brain develop.
   b The brain gets smaller and less efficient.
   c The brain grows less creative.
4 At what age are you allowed to vote in many countries?
   a 16
   b 18
   c 25
5 Why do you think people are allowed to vote at a certain age?
   a Governments want younger voters.
   b Young people are risk-takers.
   c People are considered to be mature adults at that age.
6 Why do many people look down on teenagers?
   a Teenagers are young.
   b Teenagers can be rude and they often do silly things.
   c Teenagers inject enthusiasm into life.
7 Which of these statements reflects the author's opinion about risk-taking in teenagers?
   a We should not give teenagers positive feedback because their decision-making is not mature.
   b We should pay more attention to the positive contribution that teenagers can make because of their ability to be creative and take risks.
   c We should be careful because teenagers do too many risky things.
8 Having read this article, what is your conclusion about the role of teenagers?
   a Teenagers can play an important role in shaping the modern world.
   b Teenagers have no role to play in shaping the modern world.
   c Neither a nor b reflects my view.

Try this

Do you agree with the opinions expressed in the article you have read? Write a short paragraph in which you say whether you agree or disagree. Give at least one reason for your answer.

Speaking and listening

Listen to and discuss radio calls

1 Listen to Audio 3.6, two calls made to a radio station. Each person explains a problem they have, which is related to studying. But the argument that each person gives is not as strong as it could be. Listen and make notes in a table like this as you listen. You should listen more than once.

Name of person	What is his/her problem?	Is this a good argument?	Why?
Mia			
Safir			

2 Now work in small groups. Listen to the radio calls again and discuss what advice you would give each person who called in.

LET'S TALK

Work in groups and prepare for a class discussion about things that might make teenagers feel down or stressed out.

1 First, work with your teacher to select one of the topics below or a similar topic.

- test and exam results
- not getting enough exercise or sleep
- not feeling part of a group
- having different family rules to friends' families
- family problems at home
- not understanding yourself
- feeling inadequate or inferior

2 Research your topic.
3 Decide on three main ideas that you feel will cause teenagers to be depressed or stressed. Give an example of each and a reason for each.
4 Decide on one possible solution to the problem that you will present to the class.
5 Draft your notes and improve them.
6 Finally, make your presentation. Each person in the group should speak for at least one minute. You can decide how you will share the presentation.

HINT

Think back to the article on the development of the teenage brain. Do more research in this area to look for explanations.

CHALLENGE YOURSELF

As a class, discuss the presentations that you listened to. Suggest further solutions to the problems that were presented.

You can also suggest other problem areas that you would like to debate in class.

Writing

Write a letter or email giving advice

You are going to write a letter or an email to a friend, to give them some friendly advice about staying well. This can include advice about mindfulness as well as advice about a healthy lifestyle.

Before you begin, read this extract from a letter to Mia. Look at the way the writer uses empathy to connect with Mia. Look at the pronouns, for example. Whose experience does the writer talk about?

HINT
Empathy is the ability to be able to understand and share what someone else is feeling. Empathy is important when giving friendly advice. People use personal experiences to show others that they understand them.

Dear Mia

I heard you asking for advice on the radio last night. It's tough sharing a bedroom with a younger brother or sister! Believe me - I know! It's also a well-documented problem in family life. I had the same problem and I am ashamed to say that I blamed my brother for my low grades. I couldn't allow things to carry on like that. I felt down and miserable.

But then my dad helped me to come up with a good solution. I accepted that I needed some privacy and that I also needed time to study. So I drew up an amazing plan. And do you know what the first part of the plan was? Accepting that my brother was not the problem! Then I started to get creative.

I hope that helps!
Best wishes
Xander

Try this

Think about all you have read, discussed and listened to in this unit.

1 Read the mind map below. Then brainstorm some new ideas. Draw your own mind map with eight to ten main suggestions that you could make to a friend.

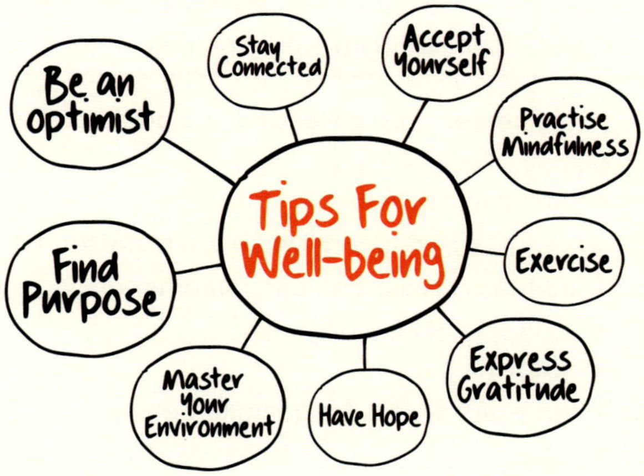

2 Write your email or letter. Choose the best four or five tips from your mind map and then explain each point in a little more detail. Try to use some of the phrases with prepositions that you have learned in this unit. Different adjectives will also make your letter or email more interesting.

HINT
Remember that you can use informal language in a letter to a friend.

Self check

Check that you:

- give friendly and good advice
- use the appropriate language for an informal letter or email
- get someone to check your spelling and grammar before you write out a clean copy
- use different types of adjectives
- use phrases with prepositions correctly.

What can you do?

Read and review what you can do.

- I can listen to and follow a physical workout podcast.
- I can talk about healthy living and well-being.
- I can read an article about mindfulness and teenage brains.
- I can write an informal text to advise a friend on healthy living and well-being.
- I can use different types of adjectives in different ways.
- I can use a range of prepositional and phrasal verbs.

Now you have completed Unit 3, you may like to try the Unit 3 online knowledge test if you are using the Boost eBook.

Review Units 1–3

PRACTISE

Use words from the box to complete these sentences.

protest	five-minute	adolescence	impulsive	widely-recognised
activist	over-tourism	best-selling	merchants	autobiography

1 The time between childhood and adulthood is called ____________.
2 Marley Dias is a young ____________, who is protesting about plastic pollution in our oceans.
3 ____________ happens when too many tourists visit a place.
4 The fitness trainer demonstrated her ____________ warm-up exercises.
5 The people of Flint organised a ____________ about clean water for their town.
6 In ten years' time, I am going to be a ____________ novelist!
7 Kelvin is ____________ for his work on producing electricity out of scrap.
8 She will not make any ____________ decisions about her future; she thinks everything through.
9 The inns were places where ____________ could rest on their travels across the desert.
10 Have you read Michelle Obama's ____________? It's called *Becoming*.

Try this

1 Work in pairs and complete this conversation. Use the correct forms of the words in brackets.

Priti: I wonder which of us (are/will be) famous in the future?

Massimo: Well, while Kofi (are/is going) to save the planet, I (will be/am) looking for a place to open my world-famous restaurant.

Aoife: So (have/has) this already been decided? Who (is/are) in charge here?

Kofi: He (are/is teasing) me. I (might/could) go to Ethiopia, where my family is from. There (may/can) be a job for me there, teaching English.

Priti: And you Aoife? What (are/will) you be doing?

Aoife: I (am/will be) fighting for women's rights, and (become/becoming) a famous actor!

Priti: And I (am/will be) raising my family.

2 When you are sure you have used the correct words, read the conversation aloud. Try to use the correct intonation as you read the statements, questions and exclamations.

PRACTISE

Complete these sentences by choosing the correct words in brackets.

1 We learned (to/about) the water problems in a small American town.
2 Many young people (is/are) collecting waste along the seashore.
3 He is the (better/best) personal trainer in our town.
4 You have to remember to (breath/breathe) while you are doing the exercise.
5 An entrance fee (are/is) paid at the gate.
6 She needs to calm (up/down), and not take things so seriously.
7 Does this bag belong (to/in) the teacher?
8 How long (have/has) he been working on his invention?
9 That was one of the (bad/worse/worst) decisions I (have/has) made!
10 Too many tourists (may/can) damage the environment.

LET'S TALK

1 Work in small groups. Look at the photographs below and read the captions.
2 Then use the internet to find out more about the places in the photographs.
3 Choose one of the places and describe it to the rest of the class. Work out how each person in the group can participate in the presentation. Use intonation to make the place sound exciting and interesting.

▲ Kerala, India

▲ Icebergs in Antarctica

CHALLENGE YOURSELF

Write a letter to a friend explaining how you have decided to take a stand about something you feel strongly about. In your letter, explain

- the issue
- your feelings about the issue
- what you plan to do about it.

PRACTISE

In Unit 3, you worked in groups to design a warm-up exercise routine. You discussed the routine, and came up with ideas which you shared with one another. Now, use what you have learned to plan and write down a 15-minute sequence of exercises.

- You should have at least five exercises.
- Number each exercise.
- Write a brief description of the exercise.
- Explain why they are in the order in which you have put them (warm up, high intensity, cool down, etc.).

You can try out your routine with your group. Are they able to follow your instructions easily? What did they find difficult to understand? How might you explain that exercise in an easier way?

4 Food for the future

In this unit you will:

- listen to a conversation about favourite foods, a podcast about **food security** and an interview with a scientist about eating insects
- talk about food you like and present your opinion on future foods to the class
- read about foods of the future and read a play script about an interesting dinner party
- write an argumentative essay in favour of or against certain future foods, and learn to punctuate texts correctly
- use present perfect and future active forms and passive forms, the future continuous forms and dependent prepositions following adjectives, nouns and verbs.

▲ A healthy plate of Irish stew

▲ An Ethiopian vegetable platter served with injera bread

▼ A selection of Indian curries, rice and chapatis

▼ Spaghetti with tomato sauce, topped with fresh basil

Speaking and listening

What do you like to eat?

1 Work in your group. Talk about the food on the opposite page.
  - a Which of these dishes have you tasted?
  - b Which do you like and why?
  - c Which do you not like and why?
  - d Which dishes are **vegetarian** and which dishes contain meat?
  - e Which dish would you like to eat right now?

2 Discuss the food of your family or culture.
  - a What is a favourite dinner for you at home?
  - b What kind of carbohydrates does your family like to eat? Choose from these or talk about your own choice.

potatoes	rice	pap	injera	naan	pasta	couscous	bread

  - c Does your family eat meat? Choose from these options and explain your choice.
    - No, we are **vegetarians** for cultural reasons.
    - Yes, but only on special occasions.
    - Yes, we usually have meat at dinner.
    - Yes, but only occasionally for health reasons.
    - No, we are vegetarians because of ethical reasons.
    - No, we don't eat meat because we don't like it.

3 Listen to Audio 4.1 as these friends talk about the food of their culture. As you listen, fill in the 'menu options' table for each speaker.

HINT
How to say the names:

Priti	(Pree-tee)
Massimo	(Mah-si-mo)
Aoife	(Ee-fa)
Kofi	(Koh-fi)

	Priti Hindi 	**Massimo Italian** 	**Aoife Irish** 	**Kofi Ethiopian** 
Name of the dish				
Meat				
Carbohydrate				
Vegetables				
Other				

Try this

Talk about the friends and the dishes that they like. Try to pronounce their names and the names of the dishes correctly. For example:

Priti does not like ..., because ...

Kofi likes ..., because ...

Speaking and listening

Listen to a podcast about food security

Learn to speak the language of food security. Food security is a phrase that means 'having reliable access to enough affordable, **nutritious** food'. This is something many of us take for granted.

1 Work with a partner. First, match the phrases in box A to their meanings in box B.

Box A	Box B
Widespread hunger and **malnutrition**	Not wasting food
Improving crop yields	Finding ways to keep food fresh and stop it from rotting
Managing the supply chain	Places which are poorer and without good roads and transport systems
Small-scale subsistence farmers	Many people going hungry and not getting enough good food
Growing more nutrient-rich food	Finding ways to get food from where it is grown, to where it is needed
Less-developed areas	Finding ways to make more food grow from a crop
Developing better **preservatives**	Farmers who grow enough food for their family with a little extra for the market
Limiting food waste	Growing good food, full of nutrients

2 Now listen to Audio 4.2, a podcast about food security. As you listen, read the phrases in box A.
   a How many syllables are there in each word?
   b Which syllables should you stress?
   c Say the words out loud to your partner.

3 Listen to Audio 4.2 again. What are the main points the speaker is making? Discuss these multiple-choice questions with your partner.

Choose the main point in each answer.

4 The question scientists have asked is:
   a How are we going to grow food for 2 billion people?
   b How do we feed 9 billion people in 2050?
   c How do scientists produce more food?

5 If we don't find an answer now
   a there will be many starving people in the future
   b it could lead to war or civil unrest
   c we won't have enough land to grow the food.

6 We need to do immediate research into
   a agriculture and its issues
   b getting fresh produce to our tables
   c improving **crop yields** and the supply chain.

7 Forty-three per cent of farmers
   a are small-scale **subsistence farmers**
   b grow enough to send food to the markets
   c grow carbohydrate crops like maize.

DID YOU KNOW?

Thousands of tonnes of fresh food is wasted every year; dumped like rubbish because it is the wrong shape or size for the supermarket shelves.

8 Most of these farmers are
  a in urbanised, richer countries
  b in India, China and Africa
  c investing money into their land.

9 The main solution to food waste is
  a preservation and drying food
  b changing our behaviour
  c improving the supply lines.

10 Listen to Audio 4.2 for a third time. Practise saying the phrases from box B to your partner again.
  a Can you make questions from the phrases?
  b Ask each other questions. For example: Will there be widespread hunger? How do we improve crop yields?

PRACTISE

1 Write down your answers to multiple-choice questions 4–9 in your notebook.

If you have all your answers correct, you should have a brief summary of the main points of the podcast.

2 Discuss your summary with your partner. Help each other to correct any wrong answers.

HINT

Once you have decided on the main ideas in your mind map, practise giving your opinion. Work with a partner. Here are some phrases to guide you.

I believe that ... (stress the word 'believe')

In my opinion, ... (stress the word 'my')

It is obvious that ... (stress 'obvious')

I agree/disagree that ... (stress 'agree' or 'disagree')

Focus on your pronunciation. Stress the words as shown, to make your spoken argument convincing.

Try this

You will work in a group of four for this activity. Your teacher will give each group a piece of paper with a topic on it. Your group has five minutes to prepare a short talk on the topic. Each member of the group will deliver one part of the talk: Introduction / two or three main points / two or three further points / conclusion.

1 Plan what you are each going to say. You can use a mind map to help you.
2 Write down key points.
3 Remember to give a reason or some evidence to back up your opinions.

Learners in a different group will use this scoring system to evaluate each member of the group's contribution to the short talk.

Speaking skills	Yes	Sometimes	No
Clearly explains their segment of the talk	2	1	0
Pronounces words clearly and correctly	2	1	0
Uses mostly accurate language	2	1	0
Uses correct stress and intonation	2	1	0
Gives own opinion, and backs it up	2	1	0

Use of English

Present perfect tense

Do you remember?

We use the present perfect tense to talk about something that started in the past, but continues in the present. We also use it to talk about our experiences up until now and to talk about recent experiences that are still affecting us.

We form the present perfect tense by adding 'have/has' to a past participle. For example:

I have been a vegetarian for five years now.

She has always hated green vegetables.

She has hurt her hand, and can't cook

HINT

To make a present perfect sentence negative, you add the word 'never' or 'not'. For example:

She had never been to that restaurant.

They have not given the scientists money for research.

PRACTISE

Write these sentences in your notebook. Choose the correct form of the word in brackets. Then underline both parts of the verb.

1 'I (has/have) never eaten meat,' Priti said.
2 'Potatoes (has/have) always been my comfort food,' Aoife said.
3 Scientists (has/have) asked that question for years.
4 (Has/Have) agriculture received the attention it deserves?
5 Farmers (has/have) spent millions of dollars on cultivating their fields.
6 The price of meat (has/have) increased in the past year.
7 I (has/have) started a small vegetable garden at home.
8 They (has/have) not tried eating new foods.

Sometimes you don't need to say who is doing the action in a sentence, because it's obvious or because you simply don't need to. This is when we use the passive voice.

To put the present perfect tense into the passive voice, we add the word 'been'. For example:

The government has declared that food security is vital. (active voice)

It has been declared that food security is vital. (passive voice)

HINT

Remember, the object of the sentence becomes the subject and the word order changes. For example:

The government has subsidised the farmers. → The farmers have been subsidised.

PRACTISE

Change these sentences into the passive voice. Remember to remove the 'doer' of the sentence and add 'been' to the verb.

1 The farmers have dumped waste food.

Do you remember?

Prepositions are words such as *on*, *in*, *at*, *with*, *for*, that describe location, time and direction.

Some phrases depend on certain prepositions for their meanings. We use these prepositions after certain adjectives or nouns to make phrases with a certain meaning. For example:

- There is a demand for fresh produce. (after a noun)
- Priti is quite good at preparing Indian food. (after an adjective)

Some prepositions are always used after certain verbs. For example:

- They argue about whether we need to eat so much meat.
- Small farmers need to be protected from big commercial farms.
- Do you believe in facts like that?

2 The government has supported small-scale farmers.
3 The World Bank has donated seed to the farmers.
4 Farmers have preserved food by drying it.
5 People have invested money in new technologies.
6 Anti-waste campaigners promote ideas for saving food.

Dependent prepositions

Talk about food security in your group. Use these questions to guide you.

1 What should scientists invest in?
2 Who should farmers be able to depend on?
3 What should governments **commit to**?
4 What should we all be aware of?
5 What do we need to do, as individuals?

PRACTISE

1 Complete these sentences using a preposition from the box.

up	about	in	from	at	with	to	down

a What do you know _________ Indian food?
b That's different _________ how we look _________ food!
c We use injera to scoop _________ our vegetable stew.
d I can't argue _________ the fact that you like bread!
e We need to invest _________ finding ways to solve the problem now.
f Fertilisers break _________ in the soil and add nutrients.
g There are practical solutions _________ these problems.
h She is not committed _________ eating only vegetables.

2 Make your own sentences using these dependent prepositions and adjectives.
a interested in
b famous for
c good at
d similar to
e different from

3 Choose the correct preposition from the brackets to follow the nouns.
a Do you have a recipe (in/for/of) the dish you are making?
b There's been a fall (of/in/at) food prices because of the grain surplus.
c Her attitude (in/of/towards) tasting anything new is terrible!
d Please give me the cheque (in/for/to) the meal.
e What's the reason (of/for/by) the change in supplier?
f I have a photograph (in/for/of) the cucumber plant I want to grow.

4 Find the incorrect use of prepositions in these sentences and correct them.
a He's very different to his sister, isn't he?
b I've been reading of a new kind of meat that's made in a laboratory.
c She wasn't the cause to all the problems.
d There's been run on of fertiliser into the river.
e They are interested about why this happens.
f It causes damage of the plants that grow between the river.

Reading

Nice to 'meat' you

1 Talk to your partner.
  a What do you think this section is going to be about?
  b What does the title tell you?
  c Can you spot the pun in the title?
  d Do you know any other puns you can share with your partner?

HINT

A pun is a play on words. For example:

She had a photographic memory, but never developed it.

The lion spat out the clown because he tasted funny.

Usually, puns make people laugh or groan!

2 Have you heard about 'clean' meat? It's also called **'cultured' meat**, and it is grown by scientists in a laboratory. Look at this photograph. Talk about these questions with your partner.

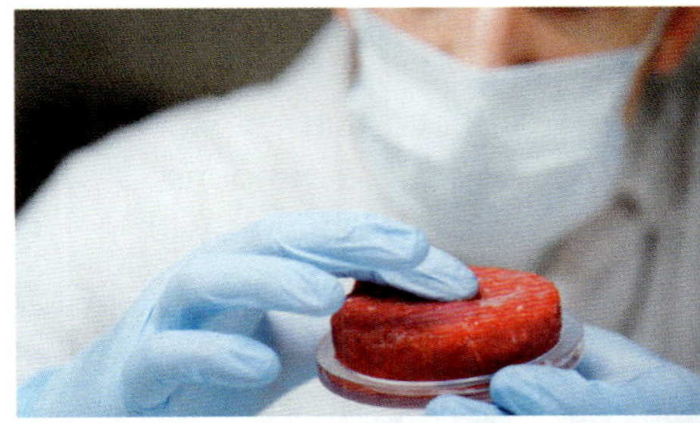

  a Would you eat this meat?
  b Is it actually meat, if it is grown in a laboratory?

3 Read this article about an alternative source of protein for people.

Scientists across the world, from Amsterdam to Adelaide, have been hard at work developing new sources of protein to feed the world's growing human population. People might see these forms of food as unnatural and feel strange about eating them at first. The question is, will people be able to overcome the 'yuck' factor and try these alternatives to meat?

We eat, on average, 80 kilograms of meat per person per year, in Europe, America and Australia. In Africa and parts of Asia, people eat much less meat – around 25 kilograms per person per year. But diets are changing and the demand for meat is growing. There is a link between money and meat too – the wealthier people become, the more meat they tend to consume.

One very interesting solution to this demand for more meat has been the development of 'cultured' meat. Cultured meat is grown in a laboratory. Cells are taken from the types of animals we use for meat, and then the cells are grown in a laboratory to establish a cell culture. The culture is then put into a bioreactor, where it grows into meat cell mush. Nutrients and vitamins are added to the mush, it is transformed into muscle cells, and then mechanically assembled into a burger patty, or another recognisable type of 'meat shape'.

For some people, this is a simply marvellous invention. You can eat 'meat' without harming an animal, and you don't have to raise animals, feed them, or deal with their waste products, etc. For others, it is a disgusting thought. They think there's something weird, unnatural and unappetising about the idea of eating a substance grown in a petri dish from an animal cell.

There are costs involved – the laboratory equipment has to be kept very sterile and clean. This is because the cells growing in the culture do not have an immune system, like an animal has, so they can be infected by bacteria easily. However, scientists argue that this 'clean' meat is the protein of the future, and hope to be able to bring it to your table by 2025.

What do you think? Will we be eating cultured burgers soon? Is 'clean' meat a sustainable way to get protein to many people? Is it meat at all?

DID YOU KNOW?

A petri dish is a round glass dish used in laboratories to grow cells. You can see one in the photograph on this page.

A bioreactor is a machine in which a biological reaction takes place.

Understanding new language

1 Learn the language of the laboratory. Look up the meanings of these words in your dictionary. Write them in your notebook. Then learn to spell the words.

laboratory immune sterile bacteria equipment scientist culture nutrients bioreactor mechanical

2 Read the article again carefully and answer these questions.
- a What needs to be overcome, to make clean meat a success?
- b What is the link between meat and money?
- c What is 'cultured' meat?
- d Do you think this is marvellous, or disgusting? Explain your answer.
- e What costs are involved in making 'cultured' meat?
- f What does 'bring it to your table by 2025' mean?

3 Put the following phrases into the correct order. Then use them to draw a flow diagram of how cultured meat is made.
- a Meat cell mush
- b Cell culture
- c Grown in a laboratory
- d Add vitamins and nutrients
- e Cells from an animal
- f Into a bioreactor
- g Muscle cells
- h Burger patty

4 Look at the language used in the reading extract. Sometimes the author implies something, without saying it directly. Here are some examples. Discuss them in your group and decide what the author means.
- a 'new sources of protein to feed the growing population'
  - Why do we need new sources of protein?
  - Are we going to run out of protein?
  - Is the author implying we might run out of food?
- b 'the "yuck" factor'
  - What is the 'yuck' factor?
  - Is it something that exists as a form of measurement?
  - Is it something that the author feels?
  - What can we imply about the author's feelings towards cultured meat?
- c There are costs involved.
  - What are the costs?
  - Who pays the costs?
  - So, does this imply that this is a cheap or expensive process?

LET'S TALK

In your group, discuss the questions in the last paragraph of the article.
- Will we be eating cultured burgers soon?
- Is 'clean' meat a sustainable way to get protein to many people?
- Is it meat at all?

Did you enjoy reading about cultured meat? Say why, or why not.

CHALLENGE YOURSELF

Do some research. Write one or two paragraphs about your favourite non-meat protein source.

Swap with a partner. Then share your ideas with the class.

How many different sources of protein did your class come up with?

Use of English

Language of the future

What will we be eating in the future? Talk about this in your group.

- Will you eat clean meat?
- Will we all be vegetarians or vegans in the future?
- What might happen if we run out of space to grow crops?
- What will our food look like in 2050? Will it just be little green nutrition pills?

Do you remember?

There are different ways of talking about the future.

You can use 'is/am/are + going to' plus the main part of the verb. For example:

We are going to learn more about other sources of protein.

You can add 'will' to the main verb. For example:

We will find a solution to the food security problem.

You can use the future continuous tense, for an action that continues to happen in the future. For example:

We will be living in small villages and eating local foods in 2050.

PRACTISE

1 Find the future forms of the verbs in these sentences. Write them in your notebook.
   - a I'm going to be cooking a vegetarian meal for my family.
   - b They will be arriving soon.
   - c We will put extra chairs around the kitchen table.
   - d It will be a bit tight, but everyone will fit in.
   - e We are going to serve them a broccoli pasta dish.
   - f My dad is going to hate it.
   - g I will be taking photographs of him eating broccoli for Instagram.
   - h I think everyone will find that quite amusing!

2 Put the words in brackets into the future tense. Write the sentences in your notebook.
   - a He (to go to) study agriculture at college.
   - b We are determined that we (find) an answer to world hunger.
   - c You (study) for at least five years, isn't that right?
   - d Yes, the course I (do) is quite long and difficult.
   - e However, at the end I (be) a highly trained agriculturalist.
   - f We (look) forward to that. You (be) very good at that job.

3 Change these passive sentences into the future passive. For example:

Transport is being organised for them. → Transport will be organised for them.

a She is being interviewed by a reporter.
b The facts are being checked by the agency.
c The agenda for the meeting is being drawn up.
d The news is being broadcast hourly.
e An answer is being sought as we speak.
f He is being collected at the airport in time.

Do you remember?

Start each sentence with a capital letter and end with a full stop.

Questions need question marks (?).

Use quotation marks for direct speech ("..." or '...').

Separate phrases with commas (,).

Don't forget to add in an apostrophe where necessary (').

Punctuation

PRACTISE

1 The writer of this short dialogue has not punctuated the text. Punctuate the text correctly.

he said i have been reading about the work they are doing on insect proteins

you mean eating insects she asked

yes he said its not new people have been eating insects for thousands of years

i know that she said but it is a new idea to people in the west i dont think scientists are going to be able to persuade people to eat insects

you may be right he said

in fact I think they would have an easier time introducing the concept of seaweed as a food stuff I think algae farming or seaweed farming is the way forward

2 Read this menu carefully to identify the punctuation and spelling errors. Now write a corrected version of it in your notebook, designing and laying it out to look like a restaurant menu.

Welcome diner's

please make your choice and let your server now what youll be eating tonite we wish you a wonderful meal at out fabulous restarant

Starter

Choice off

1. seeweed soup with lot's of spice
2. pepered ants on mangoe leafs

***

mane course

choice of

1. grilled termites on jollof rice
2. thai green curry grasshoppers

***

desert

choice of

1. fresh fruits with ice crème
2. chocholate coated grubs

Reading

Read about a dinner party

1 You will remember Priti, Massimo, Kofi and Aoife from earlier in this unit. They were planning to have a dinner party. In your group, quickly recap

- where each person is from
- what their favourite foods are
- who eats meat and who is vegetarian.

▲ Massimo will be hosting the dinner party. He said he has a surprise for everyone

▲ Aoife will be bringing dessert

▲ Priti will be bringing snacks

▲ Kofi is responsible for the drinks

2 Read this play script about the dinner party Massimo will be hosting. Read it aloud, in groups of five. Four of you take one of the parts and the fifth person reads the stage directions.

Act 1, Scene 1

The dinner party

There is a knock on the door. Massimo moves across the room to answer it. He has a gleeful expression on his face. He rubs his hands together.

MASSIMO: Priti, you're late, but it's lovely to see you. Come inside. Can I take that from you?

He indicates her shopping bag, which she passes over to him.

PRITI: Thanks, Massi. You look all excited. What's up? What are you going to serve us for dinner?

MASSIMO: It's a surprise!

PRITI: Why do I have a funny feeling about this dinner? Are the others here yet?

KOFI and AOIFE: (*together*) Yessss. (*They laugh*) Ready and waiting!

AOIFE: You'll never believe this Priti. Come in here. I hope you brought good snacks, because it may be all you'll be eating!

Priti and Massimo enter the dining room, where there is a beautifully arranged spread of food on the table, none of which looks familiar. All of which looks small. And bug-shaped. Except for the burgers.

MASSIMO: May I present to you, 'The food of the future!'

PRITI: Oh my word. What on Earth are those? Are those bugs? Thank heavens I'm a vegetarian!

KOFI: And you know how, the other day, I said at home we eat meat only on special occasions? Well, I'm almost scared to ask. Massi, what kind of meat is that? And next question: is this a special occasion?

MASSIMO: You guys are so conservative! Aren't you impressed by this future-facing, fantastic food? Come on, sit down and stop moaning, and I'll tell you all about it.

The group gathers around the table with various expressions of disgust and fascination, and sits down. Kofi passes round some fruit juice and Priti arranges the snacks directly in front of her, with her arms around them.

AOIFE: (*whispering*) Priti, I'll give you five bucks if you share your snacks with me. (*They burst out laughing.*)

PRITI: You'll be giving me a lot more than that before this dinner is over!

MASSIMO: Attention all, attention. (*He taps his spoon against a glass.*) Right. This over here is Thai cricket stir fry – quite spicy, lots of green chilli and coconut milk, but quite delicious!

KOFI: You left out the description of the crickets, man.

MASSIMO: Well, first you remove the legs and wings, and then you roast them in the oven, before adding them to the stir fry.

AOIFE: Way too much information!

KOFI: What about the burgers? If it's that pseudo-meat mush, then I'm out of here!

MASSIMO: No, one day that will be on the market, and then watch out! These are your standard vegetarian patties, for those of you who are not good at trying new things. And for dessert, I have chocolate-coated termites in the fridge.

Everyone makes retching sounds. Aoife holds up a paper bag and waves it above her head.

AOIFE: Not to worry. I brought cupcakes and brownies. All is not lost!

MASSIMO: (*dishing up a spoonful of the stir fry*) Tuck in. Crickets, anyone?

3 Now, answer these questions in your notebook.

a What is each of the friends contributing to the dinner party?
b Why is Massimo so excited?
c Why is Priti glad that she's a vegetarian?
d Describe the ingredients in the Thai dish.

- **e** How are the crickets prepared?
- **f** What does Kofi mean by 'pseudo-meat mush'?
- **g** What are the options for dessert?
- **h** Who do you think will try the crickets? Why?

4 Did you enjoy reading this play script? Talk about this in your group.

- **a** How does a play script differ from a dialogue?
- **b** Which character did you like the most?
- **c** Did any of the characters remind you of a friend? Say who and why.
- **d** Which character is most like you?
- **e** Were the stage directions helpful in setting the scene?

5 Talk about things that are implied, but not said out loud. This happens several times in the script.

- **a** '[Massimo] had a gleeful expression on his face.' What does his facial expression imply?
- **b** 'Why do I have a funny feeling about this dinner?' Something is different and Priti can feel it. What do her words imply?
- **c** 'Thank heavens I'm a vegetarian!' What do these words imply?
- **d** 'I'll give you five bucks if you share your snacks with me.' What is Aoife implying?

6 Can you find other examples of implied meaning in the play script? Work with a partner. Start with Priti's next comment: 'You'll be giving me a lot more than that before this dinner is over!'

Try this

Practise this scene of the play in your group. Be prepared to present it to the class. You can bring in props and costumes, and even food as part of the act, to make your presentation of the play more interesting.

CHALLENGE YOURSELF

What happens next? Write the next scene of the play. Who tries the new food? What kind of response does Massimo get from his friends?

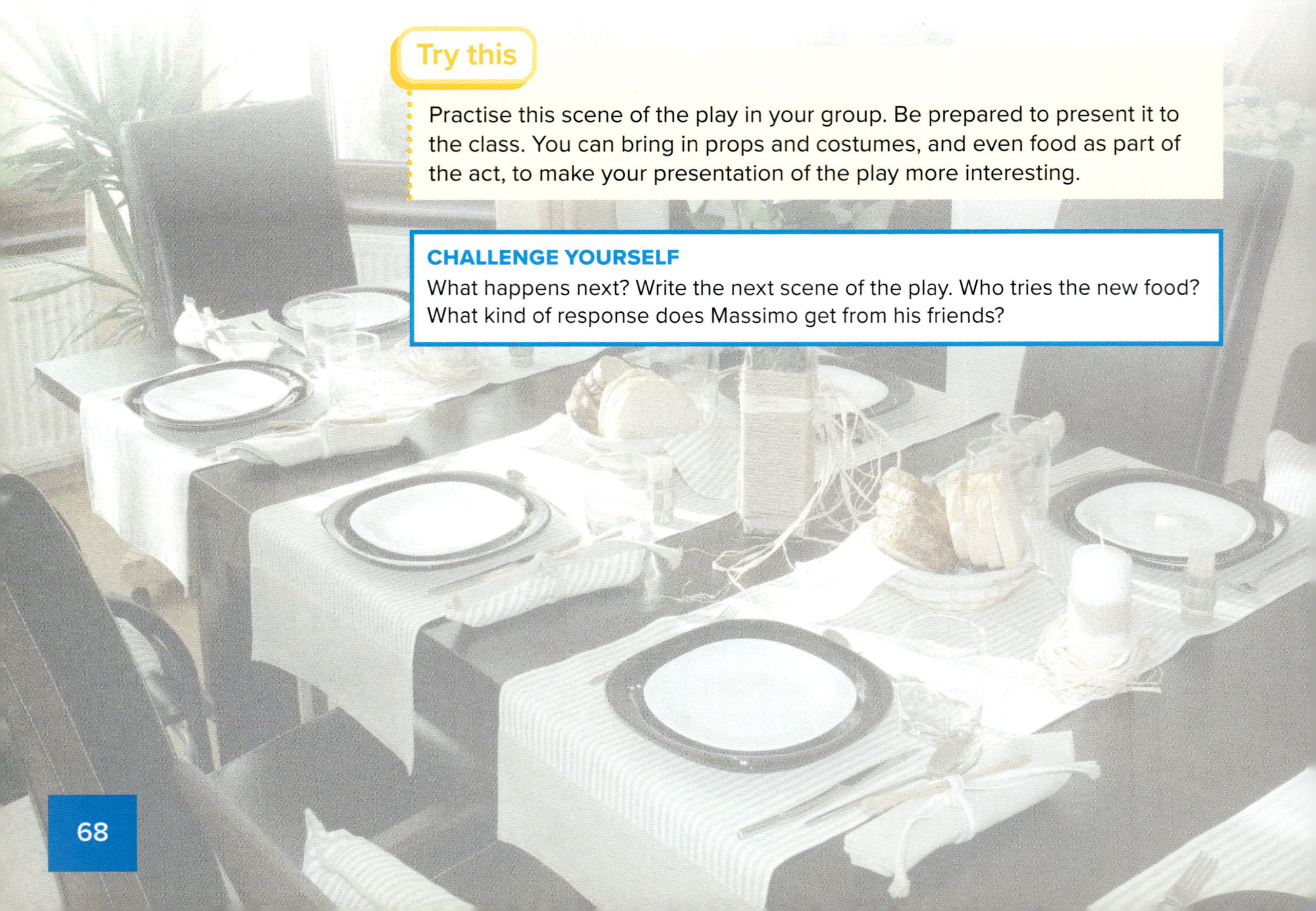

Speaking and listening

Listen to an interview

entomophagy
/ˌɛntəˈmɒfədʒi/
noun
1. the practice of eating insects, especially by people.

1 Have you ever eaten insects, on purpose?
 a What did they taste like?
 b Would you do it again?
2 What advice would you give someone who has to eat insects?
3 Do you consider insects as a food source for the future? Explain your answer.
4 Listen to Audio 4.3, Professor Anthopper talking about another source of protein for people. As you listen, find the answers to the following questions in the insects.
 a What two foods that you eat probably have insects in them?
 b What two bugs do people already eat?
 c Give two examples of insect snacks.
 d What is an easier way to eat insects?
 e What goodness are insects full of?
 f What advantages do insects have over other food sources?

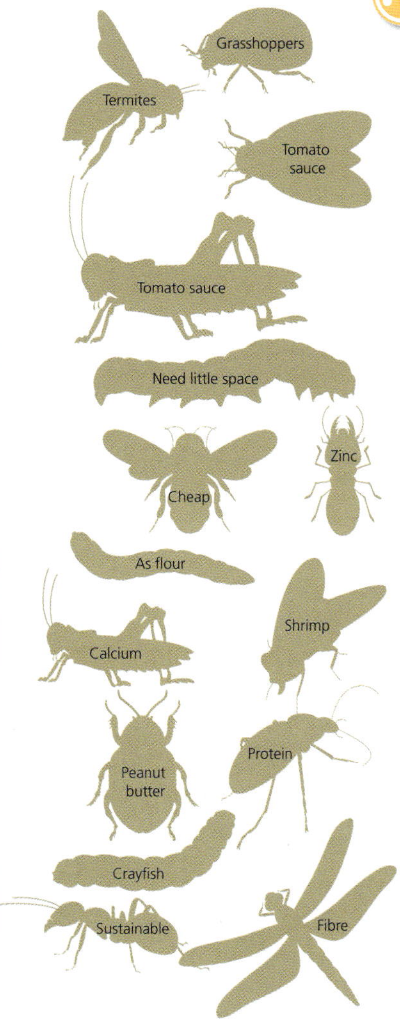

LET'S TALK

You will need a scribe, or a set of scribes, to write down your answers on the board.

1 What is the professor's opinion about eating insects? Write the main points on the board.
2 What examples does he give, to back up his opinion? (Think of the protein source, the price, etc.) Add these to your list on the board.
3 Do you agree with the professor's opinions about eating insects? Give a reason for your answer.
4 How many people in the class agree with his opinion, but would still not be able to eat insects? Can you say why? Is it the 'yuck' factor?
5 How could you persuade people that it is good to eat insects? What arguments would you use?

Write up all your persuasive arguments on the board, under the heading: Excellent reasons for eating insects.

Writing

Write an argumentative essay

▲ Meat or vegetables? Can you survive on just one or the other?

Try this

You are going to write an argumentative essay on one of these topics:

A We should all become vegetarian.
B My original solution to food insecurity.
C Meat is no longer an option as a protein source.

You can also use one of the photographs or infographics in this section as a source of inspiration for your essay, and come up with your own title.

There are several steps in writing an argumentative essay.

Step 1

Begin by planning your essay.

- You can use a spider diagram or a mind map to help you.
- Decide on your essay title.
- Put it in the middle of your mind map.
- Add legs to your diagram for each of the points that supports your main argument.
- What is your conclusion going to be? Give it a leg of its own. Your final planning diagram may look like this:

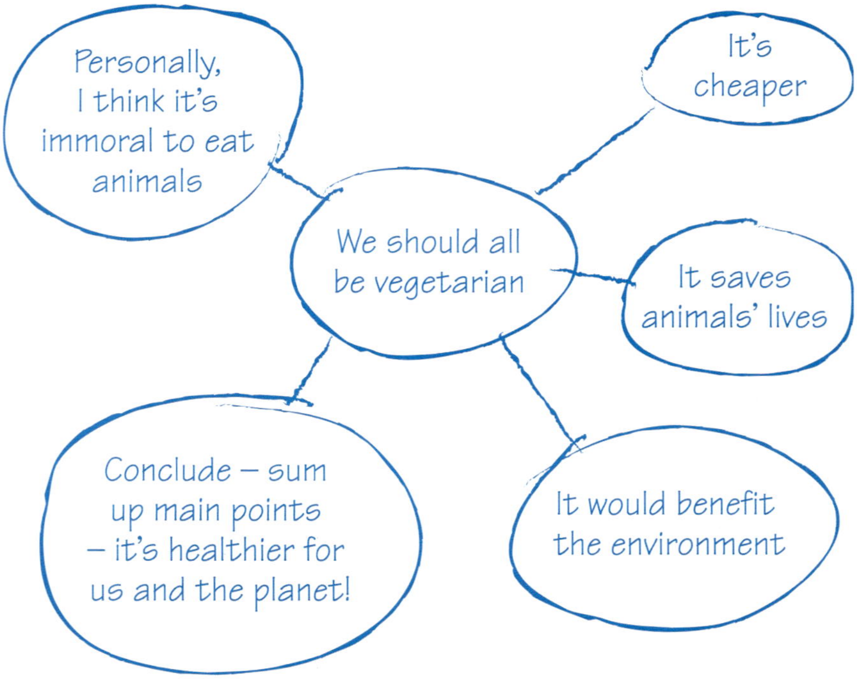

HINT

Remember how to structure your paragraphs.

- Have one main topic sentence per paragraph.
- Include two or three supporting sentences.
- Join sentences with conjunctions, such as 'first', 'then', 'finally'.
- Use a variety of sentences (different kinds and lengths).

Step 2

Next, do a first draft of your essay, based on your mind map. Remember to follow all these steps:

- Start your essay by stating your argument (paragraph 1).
- Express your opinion strongly (throughout the essay).
- Give reasons and examples to support your argument (at least three solid examples or reasons).
- Come to a good conclusion at the end (final paragraph).
- Join your paragraphs using a range of connective words like 'first', then 'next' and 'finally'.

Step 3

Swap your essay with a partner. Proofread each other's essay. Check for language and spelling errors.

Step 4

Write out a neat copy of your essay. Hand in your mind map, your rough draft and your neat copy to your teacher.

▲ The school lunchbox of the future?

Self check

Check your essay before you hand it in to your teacher.

1 Have you used the present perfect tense, in the active and passive voice?

2 Have you used a range of future forms to talk about the food of the future?

3 Have you used dependent prepositions, following nouns, adjectives and verbs? For example: *invest in*, *depend on*, *impressed by*, *involved with*, *developed by*.

4 Have you spelled each word and punctuated your essay correctly?

What can you do?

Read and review what you can do.

- I can listen to a conversation about favourite foods, a podcast about food security and an interview with a scientist about eating insects.
- I can talk about food I like and present my opinion on future foods to the class.
- I can read about foods of the future and read and act out a play script about an interesting dinner party.
- I can write an argumentative essay in favour of or against certain future foods, and punctuate texts correctly.
- I can use the present perfect and future active forms and passive forms, the future continuous forms and dependent prepositions following adjectives, nouns and verbs.

Now you have completed Unit 4, you may like to try the Unit 4 online knowledge test if you are using the Boost eBook.

5 Technology matters

In this unit you will:

- listen to personal accounts of living off-**grid**
- listen to a discussion about the effects of technology
- talk about the pros and cons of technology and of living off-grid
- read about people who have lived off-grid in remote places
- write a real or imagined account of what it is like to live off-grid in harsh conditions
- use adverbs to make comparisons
- use conditionals to talk about imagined conditions
- use causative verbs.

Speaking and listening

Technology – how useful?

Work in groups.

1 Talk about the signs on the opposite page. Do you know what they mean? Match one of the descriptions below to a picture on the opposite page.

   a A phrase from a famous book called *Nineteen Eighty-Four*. The sign means that the government is watching everything you do in order to control you.
   b Closed-circuit television consists of cameras which record activities in certain areas and display them on television screens.
   c The phrase used to describe when people do not use or do not depend on power (electricity) which is supplied by a power grid.
   d An electronic road sign, warning motorists about problems on the road ahead.

2 Now discuss the signs on the opposite page. Are they useful? Are they positive or negative? Ask each other questions to share your knowledge and ideas. Use questions that start like this:

- Where ...?
- What ...?
- Who ...?
- Is/Are ...?
- How ...?
- Why ...?
- Do/Does ...?

DID YOU KNOW?

The book *Nineteen Eighty-Four* was written by George Orwell in 1949. It predicted a time in the future (1984) when governments would use technology to control people.

Work in pairs.

3 Make a list of all the technology that you use and then make a list of the technology that you think your parents/carers and their friends used when they were your age.

4 Compare your lists with others in the class. What are the main differences between what you use now and what you think your parents and their friends used in the past?

5 Discuss these questions in pairs.

   a Do you think technology has improved your life? How?
   b Was life sometimes better without so much technology? How?

Speaking and listening

Technology – the pros and cons

Syllable stress is important because it helps other people to understand what you are saying. If you stress the wrong syllable, other people may not understand you.

There are some rules about syllable stress, but there are also many exceptions to these rules. Here are some useful rules:

- Never stress the end syllable in longer adverbs and adjectives such as '**effortlessly**'.
- Never stress the -ing syllable at the end of a verb or noun.

HINT
A dictionary can help you to pronounce words. For example, the word 'effect' is written like this: /ɪˈfɛkt/ in phonetics. You may not understand phonetics but the ' before the f tells us that the stress is on the syllable that begins with f, so we say 'eff<u>ect</u>'.

PRACTISE

1 Listen to Audio 5.1. Listen carefully to which syllable is stressed in each word.

effect affect effortlessly **efficiently** **positively** **negatively** **interacting** **distracting**

2 Work in pairs. Say the words in the box and match them with their meanings.

a (adverb) in a way that is quick and without making mistakes
b (gerund) being and doing something with someone
c (adverb) in a way that is bad
d (adverb) in a way that is good
e (adjective) taking your attention away from something
f (adverb) doing something that needs very little physical or mental energy
g (noun) a change
h (verb) to make something change

3 Make your own sentences with each word. Write the sentences in your notebook and then read them aloud to your partner.

Try this

Some words have the same stress patterns. They have the same number of syllables and the same syllable is stressed in each word. For example:

<u>po</u>/si/tive/ly and <u>ne</u>/ga/tive/ly.

Work in pairs or small groups. Write each of the words above, as well as the words in the box below, on small pieces of paper.

Place the papers in a pile face down. Take turns to take a piece of paper. Read the word on the paper aloud and identify the stress pattern in the word. Arrange the words in piles or groups according to their stress patterns. Some piles may only have one word.

technology advantages balance electricity differences television

HINT
Identify the number of syllables in each word first. Then say the word aloud to help you decide which syllable to stress.

Technology plays an important role in our lives today. It affects the way we behave, communicate, learn and think. Sometimes it affects us positively and sometimes it affects us negatively.

HINT

Find the key nouns and adverbs in the list of points on the right and listen for those words. For example, efficiently. Listen to how this word is used on the audio.

PRACTISE

Listen to Audio 5.2, an online discussion about the pros (advantages) and cons (disadvantages) of technology.

Which of the following points, according to the discussion in Audio 5.2, is a pro and which is a con of technology? Make a list under two headings: Pros and Cons. Look up any words that you do not understand.

- It helps us work more efficiently.
- It allows us to communicate much more easily.
- It is isolating.
- It allows us to store and file information effortlessly.
- It creates exciting ways to learn.
- It is distracting.
- It prepares us for the future.

Try this

Work in groups. Do you think the statements you have listed are facts or opinions? Listen to Audio 5.2 again and give reasons for your answer.

HINT

Remember that for something to be a fact, you must be able to check it or prove it.

PRACTISE

Work in pairs. Prepare a short, one-minute presentation about the effects of technology. In your presentation:

- State a general opinion. (Start like this: We think/believe that ...)
- Give two facts to support your opinion. (Start like this: In [date], ... statistics showed us that ...)

You will need to do some research in order to find facts to support your opinions.

Use of English

Using adverbs in different ways

Adverbs can sometimes be placed before the verb as well as after the verb. For example:

Everything is stored safely and effortlessly on a cloud.

Everything is safely and effortlessly stored on a cloud.

Do you remember?

You can use adverbs to describe and compare actions. For example:

You can store data more efficiently on a cloud than on a memory stick.

PRACTISE

1 Work in pairs. Can you identify the adverbs in these sentences from Audio 5.2? Which actions do the adverbs describe or compare?
   - a Technology helps people to get work done more quickly and efficiently than before.
   - b It also helps us to communicate much more easily.
   - c We don't have time to sit quietly and think for ourselves.
   - d A balance between using technology and not using technology works by far the best then.

2 Work in pairs. Complete these sentences in your notebook, using the words in brackets in the correct form as adverbs. Do this as quickly as you can to revise irregular adverbs.
   - a This is the app I use (less) on my phone.
   - b You can get (good) at this video game if you practise regularly.
   - c The red team played (bad) than the green team.
   - d Technology makes life (easy).
   - e My brother only sits (quiet) when he plays on his tablet.

3 Choose the best words to complete each sentence. Write them in your notebook.
   - a Using the internet gets your homework finished (more quickly/ more quicker).
   - b She manages to use all the latest technology (effortless/effortlessly)!
   - c I like talking to people (much more/very more) than chatting on **social media**.
   - d My parents know (quite a lot/a lot quite) about technology even though they did not grow up with it like I did.
   - e He asked us to make (slightly less/less slightly) noise as he was trying to work.
   - f Mara uses her phone (less than/the least of) all of us because she doesn't like technology.

We can intensify or make the meaning of an adverb stronger with words such as *a little*, *by far*, *much*, *a lot*, *quite*, *slightly*, *easily*. For example:

That works by far the best.

(Using 'by far' gives the superlative adverb 'the best' a stronger meaning.)

I get my work done much more quickly than before because I use a laptop.

(Adding 'much' gives the comparative adverb 'more quickly' a stronger meaning.)

Try this

Work in pairs. Read each sentence aloud. Then try out ways of making the underlined adverb in each sentence stronger.

1. How can we do this effortlessly?
2. I need to be able to sit quietly sometimes and just think!
3. My brother uses the internet positively now that he has realised it can help him with his work.
4. 'Don't distract me much. I need to finish this.'
5. He is doing the best in the computer graphics course.
6. The boys are playing more noisily than they played yesterday.

CHALLENGE YOURSELF

Look at the image below. Read the caption. Can you explain what it means?

Do you agree or disagree? Try to use some adverbs in your answers.

Switching off is good for the environment

▲ The signs in this photograph contradict each other

CHALLENGE YOURSELF

Read this short extract from the book *Nineteen Eighty-Four* (also written *1984*). Why are the names of these government ministries contradictions?

'The Ministry of Peace concerns itself with war, the Ministry of Truth with lies, the Ministry of Love with torture and the Ministry of Plenty with starvation. These contradictions are not accidental.'

George Orwell, *1984*

Reading

Read arguments

The expression 'to contradict yourself' means to say the opposite of what you said before. People often contradict themselves when they present arguments and this makes their arguments inconsistent.

1 Work in pairs. Read these short arguments and identify the **contradictions** that make these arguments inconsistent.

Addicted to technology

I love having access to messaging and the internet whenever I need it. I enjoy following my friends on social media and posting as well – it's a fun way to stay in touch. I don't feel guilty about checking social media several times a day, that seems fine to me. I don't feel guilty when I check my social media. I do really hate it when people don't reply to my messages when I can see they have read them! But I am not **addicted** to technology, like some of my friends. They all seem to suffer from FoMO – you know, 'Fear of Missing Out'! They check their phones all the time. I mean, who wants to read the news 10 times a day? Who wants to look at hundreds of boring photographs of other people eating and drinking? If only I had known what silly pictures people would post I would never have joined Facebook. It's different if you use the internet to do your homework or if you are made to do research for a project though of course. You need to spend time on that. But would my life have been better if I had not had access to social media? Perhaps.

– Dave

A digital detox

I think that technology is quite toxic or harmful at times and that we should all do a 'digital **detox**' from time to time. We all rely too much on technology. So we should go back to the simple life – grow our own food, write real letters, walk or ride bicycles instead of getting in cars – all that sort of thing. It's quite easy and there are some great websites on the subject. Check out subjects like 'Living off-grid', for example. We need to slow down. We can start by removing the annoying alerts that go 'ping' every time someone comments on our posts or sends us a message. Don't let your phone rule your life. Reclaim your phones! It makes you feel happier and more in control afterwards. Just let your friends know so that you don't feel cut off from others or a bit lost!

– Mara

> **LET'S TALK**
> Work in groups and discuss your relationship with technology. Use these questions to guide your discussion.
> - Do you think technology is essential in your lives? Why?
> - How would you feel if your access to technology was suddenly taken away?
> - Do you think you need a 'digital detox'? Why?
> - Do you think the use of technology could cause any of the following effects?
>   - insomnia (inability to sleep)
>   - being unfit
>   - blurred or bad vision (bad eyesight)
>   - injuries

2 In pairs, read 'Addicted to technology' again. Are these statements true or false?
   a Dave thinks his friends are addicted to technology because they check their phones all the time.
   b Dave does not check his phone all the time.
   c Dave contradicts himself because he doesn't see a problem with checking social media several times a day himself, but he says he is not like his friends who are addicted to technology and have FoMO.

3 Read 'A digital detox' again and answer these questions.
   a Does Mara think it is good for us to take a break from using technology?
   b What argument does Mara give to support this?
   c What does Mara say that contradicts her argument?

Vocabulary and spelling

What do the following expressions mean? Discuss and choose the best answers.

1 'a digital detox'
   a a time when you relax and enjoy technology for entertainment
   b a time when you take a break from technology

2 'to feel guilty'
   a to feel bad or ashamed about something you are doing or have done
   b to be accused of doing something wrong

3 'fear of missing out'
   a to be worried that you will feel excluded because you do not know some important information that other people know
   b to be afraid that you will be left behind and not be able to do something important

4 'living off-grid'
   a living in the country or in a place where there is no transport
   b living in such a way that you do not rely on others for electricity, water and food

5 Find and correct the spelling mistakes in these sentences. Write them in your notebook.
   a Our modern lives are built around tecknology.
   b Most people rely on social media to comunicate with their friends.
   c Do you feel gilty about the hours that you spend on social media?
   d We tried living of-grid once but we all felt quite lonely and disconected.
   e In my opinun, it is silly to try and do a digital detox when technology has so many benefits.

Use of English

Third conditional

Do you remember?

We use the word 'if' to express conditions in sentences with more than one clause. 'If' can be at the beginning of a sentence or in the middle of the sentence.

Type of conditional	Example	When we use it
Zero conditional	If you have an opinion, say it!	We use the zero conditional to say things we know are true and to talk about science facts.
First conditional	If you do not learn how to use technology, you will not be able to access information.	We use the first conditional if there is a very real possibility that something will happen.
Second conditional	I would be able to use this device, if I understood how the technology worked.	We use the second conditional when we want to say the second thing will only happen if the first thing happens.

Try this

Working in pairs, discuss the verb forms used in each clause in each type of conditional sentence.

- Zero conditional: If + ____________ tense + present simple tense.
- First conditional: If + present simple tense + ____________ tense.
- Second conditional: If + ____________ tense + would.

We use the third conditional to describe something that did not happen and to imagine the result. To form this, we use:

If + would have + verb in one clause and the past perfect tense in the other clause.

Look at these examples:

His life would have been easier if he had had access to the internet.

(This means that he did not have access to the internet and so his life was not easy.)

If only I had understood that message, I would not have made a mistake.

(This means that I made a mistake because I did not understand the message.)

If only I had known what silly pictures people would post I would never have joined Facebook.

(This means I would not have joined Facebook if I had known that people would post silly pictures.)

HINT
Read all the clauses first before you try and make them into sentences.

PRACTISE

Use a clause from each column to make six sentences that make sense.

My project would have been better	I would have messaged you.
Our lives would have been easier	if he had known the reason for your absence.
This meal would have been better	if we had built a bigger house.
If only I had seen your text,	she would not have been bitten!
If only she had brought some mosquito repellent,	if I had had access to the internet.
He would not have been so angry	if we had cooked it slowly.

Try this

Work in pairs and talk about some of the things that you regret having done or not done. Make ten sentences (five with 'if' at the beginning and five with 'if' in the middle). Make sure you use the phrase 'if only' in at least some of your sentences. Read your best three sentences aloud to the class. For example:

If only I had studied for the exam, I would have passed!

If I had bought some flour at the shop, I could have made a cake.

Try this

Work in pairs. Discuss and complete these sentences in ways that make sense. Use causative verbs.

1 We had the shoemaker ________________.
2 We let them run all night and ________________.
3 My aunt got us all to ________________.
4 The teachers made us ________________.

Some verbs (called causative verbs) describe actions that the subject of a sentence got someone or something else to do or not to do. For example:

We <u>had</u> the electric water heater in our house replaced by a solar powered water heater.

She <u>let</u> her phone rule her life!

They <u>made</u> us do research on the internet for our project./They <u>got</u> us to do a lot of research on the internet for our project.

Mara <u>got</u> her work done by switching off all her social media.

PRACTISE

Choose the best words to complete each sentence.

1 My mother (let/had) me finish my conversation before she asked me to help in the kitchen.
2 The teachers (got/made) us hand in our phones before the examination.
3 How do you manage to (get/make) all your work done so quickly?
4 I (had/got) my friend show me how to make the best fortune cookies.

Reading

Read an account about living off-grid

solar panels fire garden recycle harsh uncomfortable peaceful slow quiet

1 Look at the photographs below. What do they tell us about living off-grid? Use some of the words in the box to describe what you think life off-grid is like.

HINT

'Living your dream' means doing something you have always wanted to do.

The phrase 'sort of' is informal language which means 'partly, not completely'.

2 Read this account about living off-grid. Think about these questions as you read:

- Does the writer make a good argument for living off-grid?
- Are there any contradictions or inconsistencies in the argument?

Living our dream – sort of!

Living off-grid had always been my parents' dream. And yes, of course, they had **romanticised** what it would be like to try and be **self-sufficient**. They thought we would all be happy and that we would save a lot of money – and help to save the environment too! They thought it was a good way of being less addicted to technology. If only we had known … Our lives would have been easier if we had thought about this move before we did it.

We used to live in a big city but we moved off-grid three years ago. My parents sold our apartment in the city and bought a few acres of land about 400 kilometres away, near a small village. There was no accommodation on the land, no electricity and no piped water. But there were trees and a river nearby.

I have to admit that we had fun at first. It was a bit of an adventure – a summer holiday adventure. We lived in a smart tent and we went on long hikes and swam in the river. We planned to build a house later. We didn't really miss the internet and we didn't mind taking cold showers outside. If only we had brought some insect repellent along though! We were all covered in insect bites after just one week.

We started a vegetable garden. Great! Eat fresh vegetables from your own garden. Sounds so ideal, doesn't it? I said I would take responsibility for this. It would be easy, wouldn't it? Well, eventually my parents had to force me to help with this. I hadn't realised what a lot of work it is to prepare a garden. I had to start a compost bin too, which I didn't really enjoy, but I guess it wasn't too bad. Digging a hole for the rubbish was worse! We are careful and don't use much plastic and stuff, but still there was always rubbish – and no rubbish collection service of course either.

We also learned to trade with other people who were trying to live off-grid. I traded some of the vegetables from the garden for some bread. My mum helped one of the other families set up a water collection system and we got cheese that they made in exchange. (They had some goats!) Then we got some hens and quite soon we were collecting our own fresh eggs every day. Of course, the hens like to lay their eggs all over the place, so Dad and I built them quite a nice place of their own. It made my job – collecting the eggs – much easier.

We rigged up solar panels, so we had light inside the tent and we also had an internet connection. But all the money we saved on electricity went to buy these panels. The internet was for emergencies and for us to complete schoolwork and assignments. But solar power works well and, according to my dad, it isn't too expensive and it is easy to set up. So that was fine and we used the solar power to heat water too. We collected water in big tanks but sometimes we had to fetch water from the river. Unfortunately, solar panels don't carry buckets of water! Do you know how heavy a bucket of water is? I remember taps and running water very fondly …
Then, when the winter came, life became harder than we could ever have imagined! I think the first thing that bothered me was the fact that it was so dark. We had to spend a lot of time inside the tent. It was **claustrophobic!** Eventually, I got my parents to agree and we moved in with friends in a proper house for a while. Later, other people in the community helped us to build a more solid and comfortable house.

And we stayed. We started to enjoy living as part of a community and helping one another. Are we living our dream? Yes, in a way. Things are a bit better now. Sometimes, during the summer, our friends from the city visit us, and they think we are so lucky to be living in this amazing place. But it would have been easier if we had tried it for a short while first before selling up and committing ourselves to this type of life. Then we might have been more prepared for how different it was going to be.

Read the account again and choose the answer to each question.

3 In which way did this family romanticise this move?
- a They thought they would be happy, that they would save money and that it would be good for the environment.
- b They thought they would enjoy being away from everyone else and not having internet connection.
- c They thought that it would make their lives easier.

4 In which ways was the new accommodation off-grid?
- a There was electricity and water supplied to the house.
- b The family grew some of their own vegetables.
- c There was no electricity or water supplied to the house.

5 Which of the following does the writer give as a positive part of living off-grid?
- a Eating fresh vegetables from the garden is good for you.
- b Collecting water from the river is healthy and fun.
- c Carrying buckets of water makes you strong.

6 Which of these statements contradicts the positive statement in question 5?
- a My parents helped me to make a vegetable garden.
- b Living inside a smart tent is very comfortable.
- c My parents had to force me to help with this.

7 Is the writer's view on solar power consistent or contradictory?
- a The view is consistent because the account says it is useful and easy to set up, which is good.
- b The view is inconsistent because the account says it is expensive and not too expensive.

8 What is the writer's overall view of living off-grid?
- a It is consistent. The author does not enjoy it.
- b It is consistent. The author loves it.
- c It is inconsistent because the author likes part of it but is honest enough to say that he/she didn't enjoy everything.

Vocabulary

1 Match these words and their definitions.

Romanticise (verb) Self-sufficient (adjective) **Rig up** (verb) Claustrophobic (adjective) Accommodation Commit to (verb)	A place to live or stay Feeling unhappy or fearful of being in a small space and not being able to escape Make an agreement or decision to do something and then do it To think about somethings in an unrealistic way in which you make things seem better than they really are To make, set up or construct something Relying on yourself and not others for food, power and so on

HINT

Find the words in the text and read the sentences in which they occur. You will find clues about the meanings.

2 Use the correct forms of the words in the table above to complete these sentences.

a If you decide to life off-grid, you will need to _________ _________ living a quiet and simple life.

b Some people enjoy being _________-_________ and not relying on others for power, water and food.

c We _________ _________ a shower system, using a bucket and a rope. It worked quite well.

d If only we hadn't _________ the whole idea of living off-grid. We should have been more realistic.

e Our _________ consisted of a tent with an outdoor shower and toilet.

f I don't really like being inside in a small room with other people all the time. It makes me feel _________.

HINT

Bias is when you show support or feelings for something without having a logical reason for doing so. For example: People who live off-grid don't like modern technology.

LET'S TALK

Work in groups. Make a presentation to the class about the benefits of trying to live off-grid. Use information you have read in this unit. You can also go online and watch videos about people who have done this in real life. Listen to what they say carefully. Some people give balanced accounts, while others can be biased.

- Make a short, clear presentation.
- Each person in the group should say something.
- Try to present and explain the facts.
- Use accurate vocabulary and remember to use connectives in your explanations to link your ideas together.

CHALLENGE YOURSELF

Have a class debate about the pros and cons of living off-grid.
Use connectives to give reasons for the points you make in the debate.
For example:
Living off-grid is good for the environment because ...
Although living off-grid is ..., it also ...

Speaking and listening

Are reality shows fact or fiction?

Try this

Work in groups and make a list of all the reality shows that you know about. Ask yourselves these questions about each show.

- Why is the show popular?
- What do people do on the show?
- Is this like real life?

Listen to Audio 5.3. A young person called Matt talks about why he joined a reality show and what it was like. Then answer these questions.

1 What did Matt decide to do?
2 Where did he go?
3 Why do you think the bears in the account were made to charge at the participants?
  a to scare the bears away from the camp
  b to make the TV series seem more exciting
  c to look after the environment.
4 Name one fact about this adventure that was given in the advertisement.
5 Name one thing that was not true about the advertisement.
6 Do you think that Matt's account is biased? Give a reason for your answer.

Writing

Write an account of living off-grid

You are going to write an account of living off-grid. You can write about a video or a TV show that you have watched, or you can try and imagine what it is like to live off-grid and write how you think you would feel and act.

Try this

1. First, think about all you have read, discussed and listened to in this unit. Look at the photographs below for more ideas.
2. Then, in a group, brainstorm some new ideas. Draw a mind map with your ideas.
3. Write your account. You should write three paragraphs. Choose the main ideas from your mind map. For example:
   Paragraph 1: Say where you went, why and what you hoped to achieve.
   Paragraph 2: Describe two or three of the daily activities. Say whether you enjoyed them or whether you found them difficult.
   Paragraph 3: Draw a conclusion. Would you do it again (or keep doing it)? What would you do differently if you had known the reality?

HINT

Remember to give reasons to support and connect your ideas.

Read your paragraphs to a partner. If your partner doesn't understand something, look carefully at what you have written.

- Can you rework the sentence?
- Perhaps the grammar needs checking.
- Maybe you need connectives to link ideas more clearly.

Self check

- Have you written three paragraphs?
- Have you spelled new words correctly?
- Have you used different types of adverbs to make your writing interesting?
- Does your account use sentences with the third conditional to talk about conditions?

What can you do?

Read and review what you can do.

- I can listen to personal accounts of living off-grid.
- I can listen and discuss the effects of technology.
- I can talk about the pros and cons of living off-grid.
- I can read about people who have lived off-grid in remote places.
- I can write an account of what it is like to live off-grid.
- I can use adverbs to make comparisons.
- I can use conditionals to talk about imagined conditions.
- I can use causative verbs.

Now you have completed Unit 5, you may like to try the Unit 5 online knowledge test if you are using the Boost eBook.

6 Connecting online

In this unit you will:

- listen to a conversation between a teenager and his grandmother, a podcast about influencers and a balloon debate
- talk about the advantages and disadvantages of being an influencer, and have a balloon debate in class
- read about different influencers on social media
- write an email to a friend about meeting an influencer or a famous person
- use a range of reported statements and question forms, and dependent prepositions following adjectives, nouns and verbs.

◀ Lyn Slater is affectionately known as a 'granfluencer'. She posts on Instagram

▼ Many people like to make cookery videos and upload them to YouTube and TikTok

Speaking and listening

What is an influencer?

1 Read what Ethan has to say about teaching his grandmother.

a What challenges do you think he faces, in trying to explain social media to her?

b What challenges do you think she faces in understanding what he is saying?

Hello there. I'm about to try to explain to my gran what an influencer is. We've already done Lesson 1: How to Use a Cellphone. That was a long day.

Lesson 2 was 'How to Use WhatsApp!' My gran calls it What's Up, and she loves it. She sends me about 10 texts a day. I've had to mute her texts, in case my phone gets confiscated at school. If I don't reply quickly enough, I'll get a text, 'Hey Ethan, why'd you blue tick me?' It's quite stressful, really.

So, I am a bit worried about teaching her about influencers. This will be Lesson Number 3! Who knows what she will do next?

2 Listen to Audio 6.1, which is Ethan's discussion with his grandmother. Talk about these questions in your group.

a Do you agree that 'Insta has the photos and **memes**, and YouTube is videos'?

b How does Ethan's grandmother surprise him?

c How does an influencer make money on social media, according to Ethan?

d What examples does Ethan give his grandmother to explain this?

e What do you think Lesson Number 4 will be about?

Try this

If you have access to the internet at school, look up 'granfluencers' and 'mukbangs'. Other strange and interesting kinds of influencers are cleanfluencers, who are passionate about cleaning, and pets. Try Lionel the Hedgehog or JiffPom the Pomeranian.

PRACTISE

Learn the language of social media, or revise what you already know, using the box below. In your pairs, match each word or phrase with its correct meaning. Write them together in your notebooks.

Word	Meaning
a text	Turn off the sound of your phone so it doesn't beep when you get a message
mute	To put a message, a photo or a video onto a social media site
blue tick	To like and follow someone on a social media site
a post	The tick on your phone which says the message has reached the other person
follower	A message you type on your phone
go viral	Someone who is followed by many people because they make interesting posts on a social media site, like Instagram or TikTok
reach	How many followers one can get; how far a message can go
influencer	Spread as quickly as a virus

Speaking and listening

Listen to a podcast about influencers

1 Which influencers or individuals do you follow? Discuss who you follow, and why, in your group.
   a How many people do you follow on social media?
   b Are they interesting people, or influencers?
   c What is the difference between the two?
   d Why do you follow these people?
   e How often do you check on what they are doing?
   f How many posts do you usually 'like' each day?

2 Listen to Audio 6.2, a podcast about the advantages and disadvantages of being an influencer. As you listen, arrange the phrases below into two separate columns in your notebook – one for advantages and one for disadvantages, like this:

Advantages	Disadvantages
Lead a glamorous life	

- Lack of integrity (truthfulness and honesty)
- Paying someone to boost your followers
- Flexibility to work where and when you like
- Need to post regularly
- Free gifts
- Hard work
- Having to employ an agent to help you get deals
- Trying to get a sponsored content (sponcon) deal
- Lots of travel
- Struggle to stay up to date
- Lead a glamorous life
- Sense of community
- Keeping the attention of your community of followers

3 Can you see that the podcast only talks about a certain kind of influencer? Look at your advantages and disadvantages columns. Talk about these statements. Do you agree or disagree with them? Justify your answers by giving good reasons for your opinions.
   a The podcast is focused on people who make money from their social media presence.
   b There's nothing wrong with making money from social media.
   c You can make money and have something to say.
   d Real influencers are people who have something real to say.

PRACTISE

Use these social media verb + preposition phrases in sentences of your own. Work with a partner to make sentences then practise saying them aloud to each other.

1 post on
2 post about
3 follow on
4 upload to
5 share with

PRACTISE

1 Work in pairs.

a Copy these sentences into your notebook.

- They seem to lead a glamorous life, with lots of travel and free gifts.
- There are many advantages to being an influencer. The first is flexibility.
- Then there's the sense of community – you are involved in building a community of followers and connecting with them.
- The higher your engagement rate, or the more you interact with your followers, the better your chances of landing a good deal with a sponsor.

b Underline the longer words, mark the syllable stresses and say the words aloud.

c Mark the words in each sentence that you think should be stressed.

d Read the sentences aloud.

e Finally, listen to Audio 6.2 again and check your pronunciation and intonation.

2 Use the verb + preposition phrases below in sentences of your own. First, make the sentences with a partner. Then, write them in your notebook.

a focus on
b difference between
c similar to
d wrong with
e right about

DID YOU KNOW?

There's a funny story about a man named Joe Nicchi, who has an ice cream truck. An influencer demanded a free ice cream from him. He said no. She got angry and said she'd post a bad review of his ice cream. Joe then put up a sign on his truck saying: '$4 an ice cream. Influencers pay double – $8'.

Try this

1 Read this text.

Hi, I'm Spencer X and I am a beatboxer.

Spencer X is my professional name - my real name is Spencer Knight. I was born on 20 April 1992 in Manhattan, New York. I have a younger sister named Gigi.

I have always enjoyed music and learned to play the trumpet when I was at middle school. I first began to get noticed when my video, 'One beatboxer, 14 genres' went viral and got millions of views.

Thanks to sponsorship from the energy drinks brand Monster Energy, I was able to turn professional and now my beatboxing has been viewed by millions of people on TikTok, Instagram and YouTube.

2 Work with a partner. Tell each other what Spencer X is saying. Start like this:

He says he is a beatboxer.
He says that he was born on ...

Use of English

Dependent prepositions and question tags

Do you remember?

In Unit 4 we learned that some phrases depend on certain prepositions for their meanings.

We use these prepositions after certain adjectives or nouns to make phrases with a certain meaning. For example:

Many people look up to influencers. (after a noun)

My sister is good at TikTok videos. (after an adjective)

Some prepositions are always used after certain verbs. For example:

They argue about whether sponsored content is good or bad.

Young people need to be protected from certain internet content.

Do you agree with making money from social media?

PRACTISE

1 Discuss the different types of social media you and your friends use. TikTok, Instagram, WhatsApp? – which one do you prefer, and why? Use these dependent prepositions in your discussion, or ones from previous exercises.

similar to	post on
different from	follow on
connect with	upload to
interact with	look up
talk about	focus on

2 Now complete these sentences with words from the list.

a I use Instagram to ______ ______ my friends when I'm in a WIFI zone.
b She doesn't ______ ______ me on social media.
c They don't ______ her ______ Instagram, do they?
d How does one ______ ______ friends far away?
e My parents only ______ ______ Facebook.
f If I spend too much time on TikTok, I can't ______ ______ my schoolwork.
g TikTok isn't ______ ______ Pinterest, is it?
h Who do you ______ ______ to as a **role model**, on social media?

Asking questions about social media

Question tags are words added on to the end of a sentence, to change it into a question. For example:

You depend on him, don't you?

He will arrive on time, won't he?

He is quite famous, isn't he?

HINT

For positive sentences, use a negative question tag. For example:

He follows you on Instagram, doesn't he?

For negative sentences, use a positive question tag. For example:

She didn't upload the video, did she?

This table gives you some examples of question tags.

Verb contains the auxiliary	is	are	will	No auxiliary
Question tag	isn't he/she/it? is he/she/it?	aren't you/they/we? are you/they/we?	won't you/he/she/it/they? will you/he/she/it/they?	don't you/they? do you/they? doesn't he/she/it? does he/she/it?

PRACTISE

1 Work with a partner to form questions from statements. One of you should read out a statement from this list, and the other must turn it into a question, by adding a question tag. Make sure you each go through the full list. Use the question tags in the table to help you.

a She is a well-known influencer.
b He does not upload videos often.
c They always like your posts.
d Joe got angry with the influencer.
e He has more followers than you.
f They are not on Instagram.
g Charli is a TikTok sensation.
h Lionel the Hedgehog is famous on Instagram.

2 Change the following statements into questions by adding a question tag. Write them in your notebook.

a People follow influencers who interest them.
b Influencers can get good deals from sponsors.
c They don't always feature products.
d Sometimes they upload videos of travel spots.
e He works hard on his posts.
f It must be very tiring to find a new post every day.
g You know about agents.
h It's not easy to build your engagement rate.

CHALLENGE YOURSELF

Write a post every day for a week, about something new and interesting each day. If you do post on social media, then upload your posts and share them with your classmates. If you don't post, keep all your writing in your notebook and hand it in at the end of the week.

Reading

Read a tadpole tale on TikTok

1 What sort of activities did you do during the COVID lockdown? Talk about this in your group.
- Did you take up a new hobby?
- How did your daily routine change?
- How much time did you spend online?
- Did you post more often than usual?

2 Read this article, adapted from *The Guardian* newspaper, which appeared during the COVID lockdown in the UK.
  a What are the main points of the article?
  b Ask your partner questions about the article. Answer the questions that he/she asks you.
  c Work together to write down, in note form, the main points of the article.

TEENAGER'S COLLECTION OF 37,000 TADPOLES TURNS HER INTO A TIKTOK STAR

Hannah McSorley's videos were a big hit online and lead to a deal with an influencer agency

▲ Hannah McSorley grew an interest in tadpoles while isolating with her family at home in County Tyrone, Northern Ireland.

'TikTok tadpole influencer' is not a career path that Hannah McSorley would have learned about at school. In lockdown, however, with her GSCEs on hold, the 17-year-old has turned a very old hobby – collecting tadpoles – into an online empire that could earn her lots of money.

McSorley's daily videos of her tens of thousands of tadpoles have attracted 535,000 followers on TikTok as @baby.frogs. This lead to a deal with a US influencer agency.

'I'm honestly amazed by the following I have,' she said. 'It's just the simple things: tadpoles, frogs. People find it fascinating.'

A week into isolating with her family at their home in County Tyrone, Northern Ireland, McSorley found a patch of **frogspawn** in a shallow puddle. She took it home in a jar, thinking it was something her nine-year-old brother would find interesting.

She found more a week later, which meant she had to upgrade the tadpoles' home from some tubs to a paddling pool filled with plants and rocks.

'I always say there's 37,928,' McSorley said. 'I call it a generous estimate.'

Her project to keep busy during lockdown has become a TikTok sensation. McSorley posts videos of herself looking after the wriggling mass of tadpoles. She gets hundreds of thousands of views and many requests for help.

She has written her own how-to guide for those wishing to start their own 'journey with tadpoles'. She feeds her tadpoles boiled lettuce or spinach daily and changes their pool water fortnightly. 'A good rule of thumb is four tadpoles per litre of water,' she writes.

She recorded three casualties in 72 days. 'Unfortunately that's just nature,' she said. 'But they are remembered, and I do funerals for them.' Her heartfelt burial of one tadpole, named Fred, has attracted more than 1.8m views.

McSorley says she was a TikTok sceptic before lockdown, watching more than she posted, 'but then I found my niche of tadpole videos'. Her account has started a trend, with 34.6m views to the #tadpole hashtag across TikTok.

McSorley wants to train as a vet, but also has plans to launch an educational YouTube channel in time for frogspawn season next year. In the meantime, she has signed with the US influencer agency Markerly to grow her reach.

'I find the tadpoles very peaceful to watch. People love the wholesomeness of my videos and their simplicity,' she said. 'It's just about tadpoles living their best lives.'

Vocabulary and spelling

1 Write out these abbreviations from the text in full.

- **a** @
- **b** GCSEs
- **c** US
- **d** vet
- **e** 34.6m

2 There are many collective nouns in this passage, for example a collection of tadpoles. Complete these collective nouns. Then use each one in a sentence.

- **a** A __________ of frogspawn
- **b** A __________ of tadpoles
- **c** A __________ of fish
- **d** A __________ of birds
- **e** A __________ of books

3 Make compound nouns by joining words from the two frogs together. Now use each of your new compound nouns in a sentence.

4 Learn to say and then spell these words. If you don't know their meanings, look them up in your dictionary. Write the meanings in your notebook.

- **a** sceptic
- **b** empire
- **c** niche
- **d** simplicity
- **e** generous
- **f** estimate

LET'S TALK

Do you think the tadpole videos would have gone viral in more 'normal' times? Discuss this in your group.

- Think about other social media stars that went viral during lockdown.
- Remember, people do interesting things when times are 'normal' too, so lockdown may not have affected what people follow. Or do you disagree?

CHALLENGE YOURSELF

Make up your own collective nouns for these:

A __________ of social media

A __________ of influencers

A __________ of posts

A __________ of TikToks

Use of English

Reported speech and question forms

When you are telling a story, or telling a friend about what someone said, you are reporting what happened in the past. So you use the past tense, and reported speech.

Try this

Work with a partner. If you were talking about Hannah McSorley, you could say: 'She said she was honestly amazed by the following she has.'

Compare this to her original words in paragraph 2 of the newspaper article: 'I'm honestly amazed by the following I have,' she said.

Draw up a list of what is different between direct speech and reported speech.

Direct speech

We use direct speech to quote the actual words that someone spoke. Direct speech is always inside speech marks (either double "..." or single '...').

Reported speech

We use reported speech to say what someone said. In reported speech we change the pronouns, the tense of the main verb, demonstratives and any adverbs of time. The word order changes too. For example:

	Direct speech	Indirect speech
statement	'I have a new blog,' said the woman.	The woman said she had a new blog.
question	'Do you know this word?' the teacher asked.	The teacher asked if I knew that word. (You add if, or whether, if a question is asked.)
command	'Bring your research tomorrow,' the teacher told us.	The teacher told us to bring our research the next day.

To change direct speech to reported speech, do the following:

- Change the word order.
- Look at the verb tenses. Go back one tense.
- Look at the nouns. Change them to pronouns.
- Look at words that express time and change them if necessary. For example:

this → that, now → then, today → that day, yesterday → the previous day, tomorrow → the next day

PRACTISE

1 Put these lines of direct speech from the reading passage into reported speech.
   - a 'People find the simple things fascinating,' she said.
   - b She said, 'I always say there are 37,928 tadpoles.'
   - c She said, 'A good rule of thumb is four tadpoles per litre of water.'
   - d 'Unfortunately that's just nature,' she said.
   - e 'It's just about tadpoles living their best lives,' she said.

2 Now try these slightly more tricky ones. Be careful of time words in these sentences.
   - a She asked, 'Please could we put them in a bigger pond?'
   - b Her father said, 'I think this new pond is a good idea.'
   - c 'Today we have a big fundraising event,' the influencer said.
   - d He said, 'We hope that tomorrow you will like our new post.'
   - e She said, 'We will launch a YouTube channel next year.'
   - f 'That's enough now,' her father said.

Try this

Write this comic strip out in reported speech.

CHALLENGE YOURSELF

Rewrite this short dialogue into reported speech.

Mother: Please get off your phone now. You know Gran is visiting today.

Daughter: I just need to quickly post this.

Mother: Now, please. I need your help.

Daughter: Done! OK, how can I make today special for Gran?

Mother: You're a sweetheart. Please could you clear this mess off the table?

Reading

Dive into the world of social media

▲ Hanihanss' blog

1 a What did you find out about when you did some research earlier in this unit? In your group, talk about what you found out about:
- cleanfluencers
- mukbangs
- animal posts
- any other interesting influencers.

b Which particular influencers did you find most interesting? Why?

c You are going to look at an Instagram post, read a short blog, and read about two TikTok stars. As you read the texts and the visuals, think about the following:
- Why do they do what they do?
- What do they believe in?
- How did they become popular?

Meet Hani

Hey everyone and welcome to my blog! I'm Hani, a 22-year-old blogger and social media influencer based in London, UK. Although I have lived in London for 16 years, I was actually born back in my hometown in Somalia. I remember coming to the UK in 2003 with just one goal in my mind: making my family proud.

I guess you could say that arriving to the country a little late meant that I was a little behind my peers and could not communicate as effectively. This only pushed me and made me fall in love with reading and writing.

... I began blogging during my first year of university as part of my media production module ... I almost went into studying psychology at university instead of advertising and public relations (this is a whole other story). ... At the time it felt like there weren't many people that I could identify with online, despite following all my favour bloggers and influencers, I never actually came across many people who looked like me. I also wanted to represent young girls that are like me and show them that there is also a platform for them online.

Lots of love, Hani xxx

Answer the following questions.

2 a Why did Hani start a blog?

b Do you prefer reading her blog or looking at the Instagram post? Why?

c Do you think it's necessary to have a blog, an Instagram account, and be on Twitter? Give a reason for your answer.

▲ JiffPom on Instagram

Fun facts about JiffPom

★ He first made headlines in 2014 when he set a pair of Guinness World Records for the fastest 10 metre run on hind legs and the fastest 5 metre run on front paws.
★ In 2014, he appeared in Katy Perry's 'Dark Horse' video which had more than two billion clicks.
★ He has nearly 9 million followers on Instagram and earns an estimated $17,500 per sponsored post.
★ He won Favourite Instagram Pet at Nickelodeon's Kids' Choice Awards in 2020.

3 a What is your first thought when you see JiffPom?
b What one fact about him do you find most interesting, and why?
c Would you follow JiffPom? Give a reason for your answer.

About Self-Care Is For Everyone

Self-Care Is For Everyone was set up on Instagram in 2018 and is now a website as well. It was designed to be a safe and welcoming space to discuss mental health, wellbeing and self-care. Many therapists and healers use the site to discuss important mental health issues, and anyone who wants to is encouraged to join in, either as an onlooker or a participant. Self-Care Is For Everyone invites people to share their personal stories about mental health and self-care. Their message is that these conversations are normal and necessary. The site now has followers in more than 20 countries, helping people around the world to understand that talking about mental health is important and something that affects us all.

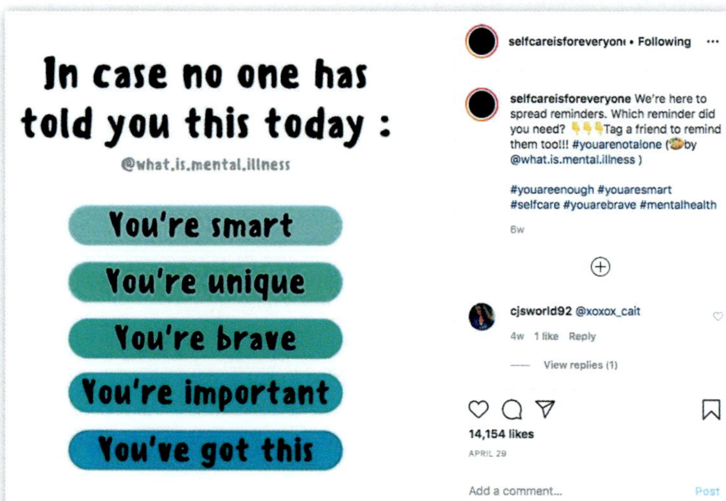

4 a Why did Self-Care Is For Everyone start their Instagram?
b What can people do on their space?
c Why is this site so necessary? Give a reason for your answer.

Facts about Maddie Moate

Maddie Moate is a BAFTA-winning presenter and YouTuber, passionate about curiosity. Maddie is one of the few family-focused 'Edu-tubers' in the UK and has been creating fun, educational, science videos for the past 8 years. She has amassed over 160,000 subscribers and over 40 million views on her videos. Maddie has her own YouTube channel, which is also the home of 'Let's Go Live with Maddie and Greg', a popular, live, science show for families and children of all ages.

In 2020, Maddie launched her podcast 'Maddie's Sound Explorers' with Sony Music. Each episode explores the sounds of science and nature as Maddie is joined by experts who guide the listeners on all kinds of journeys.

5 **a** Maddie calls herself a family-focused 'Edu-tuber'. What do you think this means?
b What do you think makes Maddie's shows and channels so popular?
c What subjects do you think might have been Maddie's favourites at school, and why?

Charli D'Amelio on TikTok

Charli D'Amelio is officially TikTok's biggest star. After launching her channel in June 2019, the 15-year-old from Connecticut rocketed to the top of the list of most popular TikTok-ers in just a matter of months. She makes short dance videos to popular songs, and then posts them. A really interesting one was the dance she made for social distancing, for the State of Ohio. It's called #distancedance.

She's now got a contract with a talent agency, and she's done a **cameo** appearance at the Super Bowl, but she has no idea why her TikTok channel took off as it did. She just started by posting 7-second clips of dance moves, and overnight, she had thousands of followers. When you ask teenagers why, they say it's because she's so friendly, and natural. And a really **exceptional** dancer, of course!

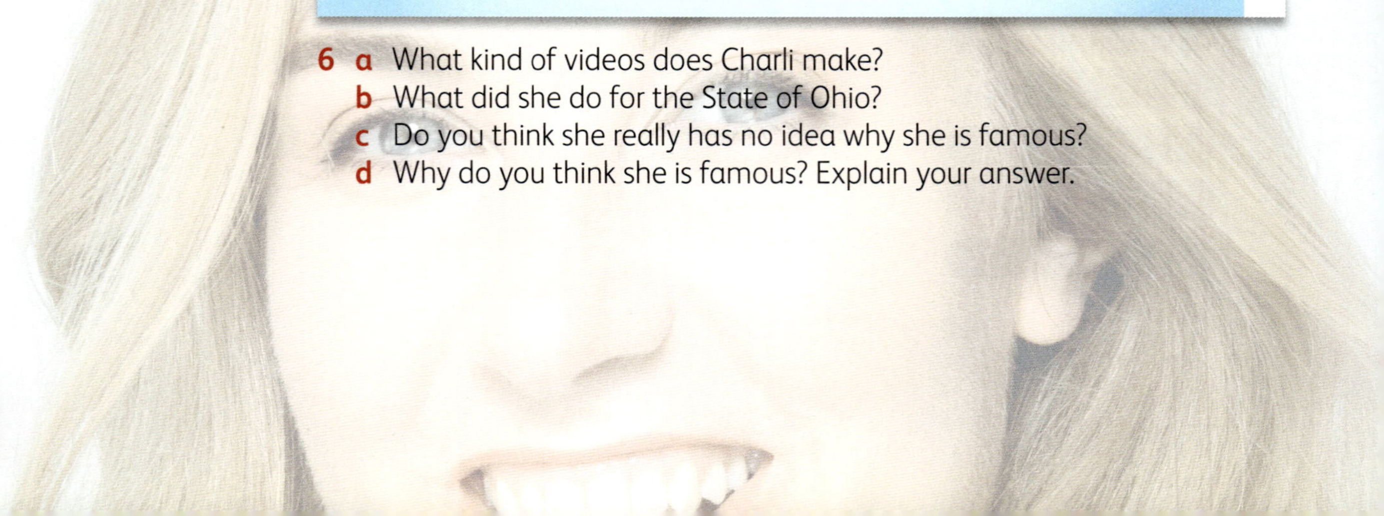

6 **a** What kind of videos does Charli make?
b What did she do for the State of Ohio?
c Do you think she really has no idea why she is famous?
d Why do you think she is famous? Explain your answer.

Speaking and listening

Listen to a dream dinner party debate

You are going to listen to part of a debate about who to invite to a dream dinner party, and then have your own dinner party debate in class. This is how the debate works:

You are hosting a luxury dinner party, but you have only four seats at the table. There are four people you would like to invite, but you can only ask three of them. Who would you choose to invite, and why?

On the list are a famous musician, a YouTube influencer with 3 million followers, a scientist who is developing the foods of the future and a powerful world leader.

1 Listen to the dream dinner party debate in Audio 6.3. Take note of the assessment criteria in the table below. You are going to give each speaker a score out of 10 to decide which guests should be invited. The guest preferred by the speaker who receives the fewest points will not be invited.

Criteria	Description	1 point	2 points
1 The opinion of each speaker	Well developed		
2 Whether they can justify their opinion	Gives good examples		
3 How well they link their ideas together	Uses joining words like: first, then, in conclusion		
4 Whether their argument makes a coherent whole	Yes, it is one main idea, well-argued		
5 Whether they listen to the opinions of others	Yes		

2 Who will not be invited?

a Take two minutes, on your own, to decide which person will not be invited. Write down your choice.

b Next, in your group, each person should state their point of view on who should not be invited. Each view must be backed up with a good reason. Your teacher will appoint a scribe to keep a tally on the board.

c Once everyone has had a chance to speak and vote for who they think should not be invited, your teacher will add up the votes. Who is the person who will not be invited to the dinner party?

3 Work in groups of five on your own debate – this time you have to pick your own people. Which four people will you choose to invite to your luxury dinner? You should each pick one person you admire because they are so interesting, or they have done so much, or will be able to do so much, for the world. Make sure you all pick different people. Now each of you argues that your person should be included on the invitation list. Then have a vote and vote one person off the list.

Writing

Write an email and a letter

You are going to write an email to a friend of yours, telling them about meeting a celebrity or an influencer. This could be an online interaction or a face-to-face meeting.

You can use any of the influencers in this unit or one of your own choice. If you have internet access, go to the individual's TikTok channel or Instagram page and follow them, to find out more about them.

Try this

Here is the computer screen, ready for you to type up your email.

Put the person's email address after To.

Add a subject in the Subject line, for example: You will never believe this!

Write the body of your email here.

Press Send after you have checked your spelling and grammar.

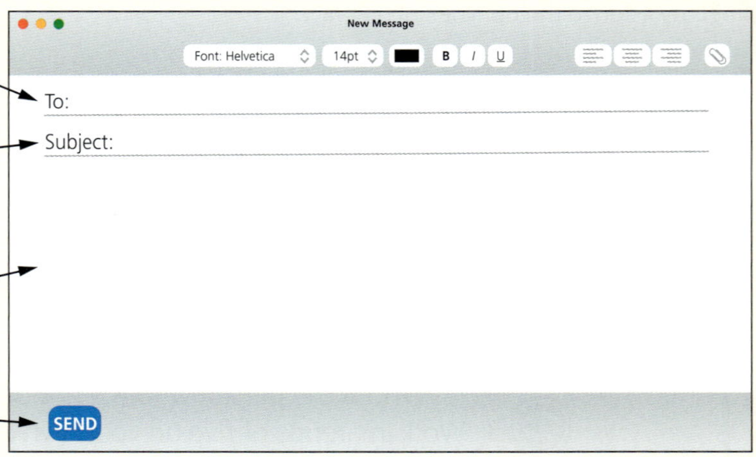

HINT

This is an email to a friend, so you can use less formal language, with some slang. A formal register would sound very strange!

Self check

Check your email before you send it to your friend.

- Have you filled in the correct address?
- Have you given your email a subject?
- Have you used dependent prepositions in your email. For example: post on, follow on, upload to, impressed by, nervous about?
- Have you used reported speech to tell your friend what the influencer/famous person said to you? For example: She told me that she was pleased to meet me!
- Did you sign off, and say goodbye?
- All done? Good, now press Send.

Try this

Write a two-paragraph open letter to a group of influencers, reminding them of their responsibilities as a group of influential people and asking for their help in raising awareness of a particular issue. Choose a current issue that you would like them to highlight, for example the fight against malaria or issues related to poverty or pollution.

- Remember to use the structure of a formal letter. If you need a quick reminder, look on page 20 of Unit 1.
- You need to use formal language and as many of the new grammar structures as you can, from this unit.
- Plan out what you want to say, in a mind map, or a quick list of important points.
- In the first paragraph, explain the problem you would like them to address. Give them your opinion on the problem.
- In the second paragraph, give your suggested solution to the problem – they could raise awareness, for example, or start a crowd-funding exercise to help. You could imply, politely, that they have a duty to assist.
- Remember to sign off (also politely).

What can you do?

Read and review what you can do.

- I can listen to a conversation between a teenager and his grandmother, a podcast about influencers and a balloon debate.
- I can talk about the advantages and disadvantages of being an influencer, and have a balloon debate in class.
- I can read about different influencers on social media.
- I can write an email to a friend about meeting an influencer or a famous person.
- I can use a range of reported statements and question forms, and dependent prepositions following adjectives, nouns and verbs.

Now you have completed Unit 6, you may like to try the Unit 6 online knowledge test if you are using the Boost eBook.

Review Units 4–6

PRACTISE

Use words and phrases from the box to complete these sentences.

quite a lot	cultured	technology	effortlessly	the best	addicted to
subsistence	malnutrition	fame	by far		

1 My brother insists he's not _____________ social media.
2 That vegetarian restaurant has _____________ burgers in town!
3 _____________ farmers grow enough food to feed their families.
4 Priti's grandmother says young people depend on _____________ too much. They can't exist without their cell phones and computers!
5 Charli dances so _____________ on her TikToks.
6 In countries where hunger is a concern, _____________ needs to be addressed by government.
7 'No, I don't think a vegetarian can eat _____________ meat; it's still meat, after all,' he said.
8 She is very rude about 'instant _____________' on social media; she says it won't last.
9 'This is _____________ the best meal I have had in an Italian restaurant,' she said.
10 There is _____________ of food left over; can we donate it to an organisation?

Try this

Work in pairs and write this conversation out as reported speech. Remember to pay attention to time words, like today, tomorrow, and to the tense of the verbs in your sentences. It is reported speech, so the verbs will be in the past tense, as you are telling someone what has happened.

Massimo: Would you like to come to dinner tomorrow, everyone?

Priti: That would be lovely. I will bring dessert.

Aoife: I will bring my fantastic company. That's all I can offer at this time.

Kofi: Let me get the drinks.

Massimo: Excellent. I will see you all tomorrow night at 7. Don't be late!

PRACTISE

Complete these sentences correctly. You will need to choose the correct words from the brackets to do this.

1 '(Are/is) you going to pay?' the waiter asked.
2 Do you depend (on/in) your cell phone for the latest posts on social media?
3 An entrance fee (is/will be) charged as a contribution to the work we do.
4 There are practical solutions (to/for) these problems.
5 We need to move (more quickly/most fast) to solve global warming.
6 Our teacher (got/made) us write an essay about our feelings about hunger.
7 'Go (ahead/about), I'll catch up later,' she said.
8 They (are/will be) coming to join us for dinner.
9 It is (much/very) more important to interact with family, rather than technology.
10 If only we had started earlier, it (will/would) have been easier to finish the work.

LET'S TALK

Work in small groups. Look at the social media screenshots in Unit 6 and read the information. Use the internet to find out more about one of the influencers and report back to the class.

- Choose one of the influencers and explain their background, what they do and how they became an influencer. (You can also choose your own influencer, if you prefer.)
- Decide how each person in the group can participate in your report back to the class.
- Remember to use intonation and implied meaning to make your information more interesting.

PRACTISE

In Unit 6, you wrote an email to a friend about meeting a celebrity or influencer. Use the same structure to write an email to a friend explaining to them your food beliefs, and why you would choose to eat or not eat certain foods.

Draft a short email of two paragraphs. You can use the following structure:

- Paragraph 1: Explain briefly what your food beliefs are.
- Paragraph 2: State why you would/would not eat certain foods.

You can send your email to a classmate, and they can write a reply.

CHALLENGE YOURSELF

Write a magazine article in which you explain why living 'off-grid' is the trend of the future.

7 Space travel

In this unit you will:

- listen to an argument about space **exploration**, to information about useful inventions that come from space travel and to a radio interview about **extra-terrestrial** life
- talk about space travel and the possibility of extra-terrestrial life, and tell the story of an encounter with an 'alien'
- read about a space trip to Mars and a film review of a **sci-fi** film
- write a story about a voyage to Mars or about living on Mars
- use a range of active and passive past perfect simple forms, past perfect continuous forms and relative clauses, including 'which' to refer to the previous clause.

▼ We have lift-off!

Speaking and listening

We have lift-off!

1 Talk about space travel in your group.
- Have you ever watched a rocket launch on TV?
- Can you describe the launch to your group? Use some of the words in the box in your description. You can also use the photographs for inspiration. Start like this:

The first thing I noticed …
Then, the …
The most incredible moment was …

lift-off	engines	launch	countdown	ignition	power	steam	flames

2 Listen to Audio 7.1, an argument between two young people who clearly have different views on space exploration.
As you listen, choose the correct answer to each of the multiple-choice questions below. Write the answers in your notebook.

3 Mei believes that
a rich people should pay for space exploration
b rich people can do whatever they like with their money
c there's going to be a space competition organised by rich people.

4 Cheung is angry because
a he thinks people should spend money on solving global warming not on space exploration
b he hates rich people
c he thinks space exploration is immoral.

5 When Cheung says 'before rich people start playing with space', he is implying that
a space exploration is not a game; it's a serious business
b rich people play all sorts of games
c there should be rules for space games.

6 Mei argues that
a academics should be involved in space exploration
b the problem is still imaginary, as it hasn't happened yet
c academics work with government and space agencies.

7 Where does Cheung's argument go wrong?
a He starts talking about other challenges that have gone wrong.
b He uses examples of accidents which have nothing to do with the topic to support his argument.
c He gets too excited and Mei tells him to calm down.

Try this

Should people be investing in space travel or not? Prepare a short talk giving your opinion.
- Start by stating your belief:

I believe that we should …

- Then, give at least three examples or reasons to back up your opinion.
- End with a strong conclusion.

Speaking and listening

The advantages of space travel

Sunglasses, baby milk formula, the camera on your smartphone – these are just some of the inventions we have because of space travel. You are going to listen to an audio about the advances we have made with other technologies, because of our attempts to travel into space.

As you listen to Audio 7.2, look at the pictures and the captions below. Match each picture to the correct caption, writing the picture number and the corresponding caption letter in your notebook.

A In the 1990s, a team at the Jet Propulsion Laboratory invented scientific-quality cameras, which are small enough to fit on a spacecraft. About a third of all cameras used in smartphones today use this technology.

B Scratch-resistant lenses had been invented by the Lewis Research Centre, when it was discovered that the same technology would work perfectly in sunglasses.

C Those puffy, well-fitting trainers? They would not exist without the soft foam developed by NASA, which was used to construct space suits.

D Foil blankets are essential in survival situations, as they trap heat and keep the person they are wrapped around warm. They were invented by NASA to protect spacecraft and people in space.

E In the 1960s, NASA invented a way to purify water in space, so the astronauts could drink it. This same technology is now used to kill bacteria in swimming pools.

F Baby milk formula now contains a nutritional enrichment ingredient, which was developed by NASA when they were exploring the use of algae as a food supplement to be used during long-duration space travel.

G NASA invented wireless headsets to allow astronauts to be hands-free, while they communicated with command central.

H NASA had to develop shock-absorbers built into robotic limbs, which were needed for their extra-vehicular activities, such as making repairs outside the spacecraft or exploring the surface of new moons and planets. This technology was adapted to create better artificial limbs.

DID YOU KNOW?

NASA (pronounced ná sa), stands for National Aeronautics and Space Administration.

PRACTISE

1 Discuss these questions in your group. Write the answers in your notebook.
  a How do inventions spread from one 'industry' to another? Look at B and C, for example.
  b What dangers are there in space? Why did NASA have to develop foil blankets (see D)?
  c Why would you need to have a water-purification system on a spacecraft (see E)?
  d Why do you think NASA prepared for 'long-duration' space travel (see F)' if astronauts were only going to the moon?
2 Say these compound words out loud. Make sure you put the stress in the correct place.

headset	sunglasses	spacecraft
hands-free	scratch-resistant	well-fitting

3 Can you say which of these words are adjectives and which of them are nouns?
4 Use each word in a sentence of your own. Write the sentences in your notebook.

Try this

Which of the technologies mentioned on these pages have you used? Discuss them in your group. Use some of the new words you have learned in your discussion, for example:

I have scratch-resistant sunglasses that I wear in summer.

CHALLENGE YOURSELF

Do some more research on one of the other technologies that came about because of space travel. Choose from this list.

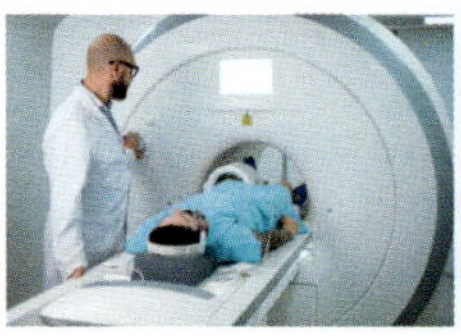

▲ CAT scans

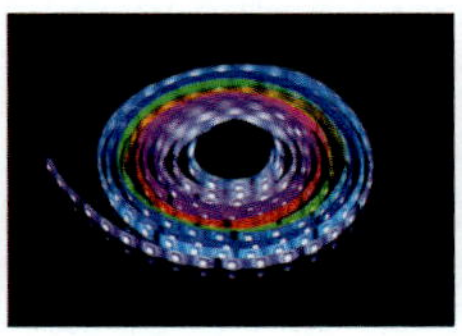

▲ LEDs

▲ Landmine removal

▲ Dust busters

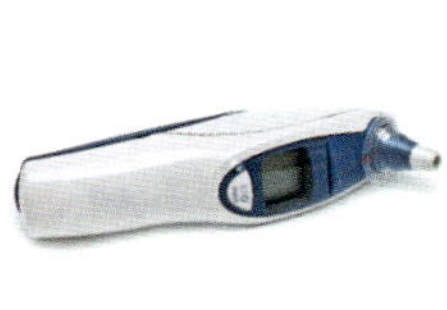

▲ Ear thermometers

▲ Home insulation

▲ The 'jaws of life'

▲ Freeze-dried food

Be ready to give a one-minute presentation to the class during your next lesson, about the invention you researched.

Use of English

Living in space

Astronauts had to deal with many challenges in space. When they had been exercising in a gym on earth, they could not imagine what it would be like exercising in space. If they had been working out on a treadmill before they went to space, they would not have had to tie themselves onto it. Can you imagine how strange it would have felt if when you had woken up in the morning you found you were strapped to your bed?

Do you remember?

We use the past perfect tense to describe an action that has been completed at some stage before, in the past. To form the past perfect tense, you use had + the past participle. For example:

He had met the astronaut before.

We use the past perfect continuous tense to show that an action that started in the past carried on until another time in the past. To make the past perfect continuous tense you use had been + the present participle. For example:

He had been floating through space for some time, before they called him back.

PRACTISE

1 In each sentence, put the verb in brackets into the past perfect tense. Remember, use the form had + ________ed. (Some of the verbs are irregular, so don't get caught out!)

- a He (exercise) in a gym in the past.
- b She (work out) on the rowing machine, then she ran on the treadmill.
- c I (wake up) already when the alarm went off.
- d He (work) on the Space Station previously.
- e They (see) that **asteroid** formation before.
- f We (make) a plan to watch the launch on TV.
- g She (buy) scratch-resistant glasses, which she lost.
- h NASA (say) the launch would happen at 8 a.m.

2 Now, put the verbs in the sentences below into the past perfect continuous tense. Remember, use the form had been + ________ing.

- a The astronaut (train) to do a spacewalk.
- b They (monitor) the events outside the spaceship.
- c They (lose) power, so something had to be done.
- d The group (eat) when they were interrupted by the captain.
- e He (try) to get their attention for a while.
- f It (rain) the night before.

Speaking space talk

To make a question in the past perfect tenses, you put the verb first. For example:

> Had he been trying to close the valve for a while?

To make a sentence negative in the past perfect tenses, you add not. For example:

> He had not closed the valve properly. / He hadn't closed the valve properly.

▲ Eating a meal can be a challenge in zero gravity!

PRACTISE

1 Turn these sentences into questions.
   a They had worked on the problem previously.
   b They had met at training camp.
   c NASA had built the spacecraft on site.
   d They had been fixing the problem when the call came in.
   e She had been talking about that very problem!
   f You had been studying aeronautics.

2 Make these sentences negative.
   a NASA had sent them all for training.
   b He had studied the maps before the trip.
   c They had strapped themselves in.
   d The spaceship had taken off.
   e Jane had flicked all the switches to green.
   f The controller had given the signal for lift-off.

We use the passive voice in the perfect past tense to talk about something that happened in the past, where the doer of the action is obvious or understood.

	Active voice	Passive voice
Past perfect	NASA had planned the launch years in advance.	The launch had been planned years in advance.

The passive voice is used:

- when you don't need to say who does the action
- if you don't want to say who the subject is, especially in formal texts.

PRACTISE

Change these sentences into the passive voice.

1 The space agency had scheduled the launch a year before.
2 The trainers had taught the astronauts how to operate the craft.
3 The chef had prepared the meals in advance.
4 The head of staff had promoted the astronaut to captain.
5 The managers had sold all the junk metal to clear space.
6 The research team had planned the trip very carefully.

Reading

Missions to Mars

1 Meet Curiosity, the NASA Rover that is currently exploring Mars. Talk about these questions in your group.
   - a Why do you think the rover was named Curiosity?
   - b What are the thick treads on the tyres for?
   - c What is the purpose of the box with the circular glass?
   - d What do you know about the exploration of Mars? Share your knowledge with your group.

2 Read the text about the many missions to Mars that have captured the attention of the world.
   As you read, decide whether each of these statements is a fact or an opinion. Make some notes in your notebook as you read.
   - a There is water under the surface of Mars.
   - b The author is biased in favour of Elon Musk.
   - c Sending a car into space on top of the SpaceX rocket was a giant ego trip.
   - d People can build a sustainable city on Mars.
   - e Elon Musk plans to build 1000 Starships to carry people and goods to Mars.
   - f The Earth's and Mars' **orbits** only align every two years.
   - g It is ridiculous to spend trillions of dollars on Mars exploration, when we could fix things on Earth.
   - h Mars is not a viable option as a second 'Earth', according to the author.
   - i We need a 'backup' planet in case of catastrophe.
   - j The Pew survey shows people believe NASA should fix problems on Earth first.

Missions to Mars

Over the last 40 years, the international space community has sent many missions to Mars. NASA has a rover on Mars at the moment, that is called Curiosity. Curiosity has been on Mars for several years now. It is beaming all sorts of interesting information back to Earth. The rover recently found tiny **organic** molecules, and some methane in the **atmosphere**, which are both positive signs of life. In late 2019, the European Space Agency's Mars Express rover found liquid water buried in the south polar region of Mars.

DID YOU KNOW?

The 'Space Race' began during the Cold War between Russia and the USA in the 1950s. The two superpowers competed in building and collecting nuclear weapons, and in trying to get a person into space first.

▲ An artist's painting of NASA's Mars Ice Home idea: Mars explorers will need shelters to protect them from the harsh Martian environment and provide a safe place to call home

What's really interesting about the missions to Mars is how many people and governments are in the race. The most famous individual involved is probably Elon Musk, who runs SpaceX. You probably remember his highly public launch of the Falcon Heavy rocket, with his red Tesla car mounted on top of it? There was a **mannequin** dressed up as Starman in the car, and Davie Bowie's music was playing loudly. SpaceX hoped to shoot the rocket, plus car, straight to Mars. Unfortunately, it overshot its orbit, and is now 88 million miles from Mars.

That did not deter Elon Musk one bit. He has a timeline and very clearly stated vehicle requirements, and he is determined both to reach Mars, and to set up a sustainable city there, in which people can live. That's his long-term vision – making humans an interplanetary species.

To do this, Musk needs to build and fly 1000 Starships, according to his estimates, which will transport cargo, infrastructure and crew to Mars over the course of 20 years.

One small snag – Mars and Earth are only close enough to each other for a two-month period, every two years. So, SpaceX would need to send off three Starships a day in this time period, in order to achieve Musk's dream.

At what cost, the critics ask? Mars has no breathable atmosphere, and no easy supply of water. Why spend trillions trying to make an **inhospitable** planet home, when we have so many problems to fix on Earth?

Elon Musk has argued that we need a 'backup' planet, in case something catastrophic happens to Earth, like an asteroid **collision**. Not everyone agrees with him. A survey organised by Pew Research Centre found that most adults in the USA believe that NASA's number one priority should be fixing things on Earth. The trillions of dollars it would take to colonise Mars could be used to find forms of renewable energy to address climate change, or even to build a system to deflect the asteroids Musk talks about.

And what about the damage we could do to Mars? What Earth microbes could astronauts introduce, that may be harmful to the life that exists on Mars? Could our efforts to find life on Mars actually kill that life off?

LET'S TALK

Talk to your partner about your fact/opinion list.

- Do you have the same answers?
- Where do you disagree? Discuss each point on which you disagree. Can you come to one opinion?
- Do you have any examples where it is a fact that someone has an opinion on?

CHALLENGE YOURSELF

You are going to be writing a story in the final lesson of this unit. It's time to begin preparation for that now. Choose **one** of these two topics:

- My journey to Mars
- Living on Mars

Start researching the practicalities of your story now. You can begin by discussing this in a group, or with a friend, so you can share ideas. You need to decide or invent

- a way of breathing on Mars and during your journey to get there
- ways of finding/growing/storing food for life
- how to travel on Mars – with what vehicle and what fuel
- other ways of living, which will be different from Earth.

Write down your ideas in point form in your notebook.

Use of English

It's all relative

Relative clauses add extra detail to a sentence. The detail they add is not essential to the meaning of a sentence, but it fills out what we know.

The laboratory invented cameras which are small enough to fit onto a spacecraft.

This is the main information. (The laboratory invented cameras)
This gives us extra information. (which are small enough to fit onto a spacecraft)

Can you find the relative clauses in these sentences? Discuss them with a partner.

- Trainers use soft foam, which was invented by NASA for space suits.
- Scratch-resistant lenses, which were invented by the Lewis Research Centre, are used in sunglasses.
- Baby milk formula contains a nutrient which was developed by NASA.

The relative pronouns are who, which and that. Relative pronouns introduce relative clauses. These clauses tell us more about people and things.

A relative clause is a part of a sentence, introduced by a relative pronoun, which has a subject and a verb, but cannot stand on its own. For example:

John Glenn, who was an astronaut, was one of the only people to land on the moon.

The Space Station, which was developed by NASA, is in orbit around Earth.

SpaceX is a space exploration business that Elon Musk built.

In each of these examples, the relative clauses are underlined. You can see that

- they are introduced by a relative pronoun
- they have a subject and a verb, but they do not have meaning on their own.

PRACTISE

1 Work with a partner. Fit the missing relative clauses from the box into these sentences. Once you have decided which piece fits which sentence, write them all in your notebook.

a Cheung thinks people __________ should spend it on worthwhile projects.
b Mei talks about other space inventions __________.
c The lab invented cameras __________.
d NASA has a rover __________.
e Organic molecules and methane have been found, __________.
f Elon Musk, __________, is quite famous.

g He is determined to set up a sustainable city ___________.
h He is going to build 1000 Starships ___________.

that is called Curiosity	in which people can live
which will transport people and cargo to Mars	who runs SpaceX
who have a lot of money	which are both signs of life
that have improved our lives	which are small enough to fit into your phone

HINT
Use *who* for people, *which* for places and things, and *that* for either people or places and things.

2 Add *'who'*, *'which'* or *'that'* to these sentences to complete the relative clauses.
a Richard Branson, ______ runs Virgin Galactic, is also involved in the space race.
b NASA, ______ has been the main US contender, has a new Mars rover.
c The launch, ______ will cost $2 million, will happen today.
d Starships ______ were invented by SpaceX, will fly three times a day.
e These ships, ______ will carry cargo and people, will be reusable.
f Robots can carry out research ______ humans would not be able to do.
g People ______ are against space travel want the focus to be on fixing Earth first.
h They say, which makes sense, that we could build a bunker on Earth, ______ would be safer than moving to Mars!

Try this

Work with a partner. Use relative clauses to describe what is happening in this photograph. Start like this:

The oranges and lemons, which ...

The astronaut, who ...

The lack of gravity, which ...

CHALLENGE YOURSELF
Look at the notes for your story, which you started making in the last lesson. See if you can make them more interesting, with more detail, by adding relative clauses. For example:

The transport system, which ...

The Food Manager, who ...

When you breathe out, the breathing system, which ...

Reading

Review a science-fiction movie

1 Have you seen any of the Star Wars movies? Talk about this in your group.
- Which movie was your favourite, and why?
- Who is your favourite character, and why?
- Which movie would you recommend to your friends?
- Try to persuade one of your friends to see your favourite movie with you, based only on your enthusiastic review of the movie.

2 Read this review of the last Star Wars movie. As you read, make short notes of the phrases that demonstrate the reviewer's opinion of the movie.

Star Wars: The Rise Of Skywalker Movie Review

By Ruby Walker

Star Wars: The Rise Of Skywalker Story: The final chapter of the Skywalker saga

The Star Wars saga continues, following on from the events of 'The Last Jedi'. Rey (Daisy Ridley), Poe Dameron (Oscar Isaac) and Finn (John Boyega) battle Kylo Ren (Adam Driver) and the First Order. 'The Rise of Skywalker' is the third and last chapter in the Skywalker line of stories in the 'Star Wars' franchise.

Star rating: ★★★½☆

The biggest challenge for the new **trilogy** is that it is supposed to bring a neat ending to the original characters – Luke Skywalker (Mark Hamill), Han Solo (Harrison Ford) and Leia Organa (Carrie Fisher) as well as to the new characters introduced in this latest trilogy.

This is not an easy task as the cast is huge, and the full series of films now covers 42 years. I'm a passionate fan, and I saw the first movie at age 7, but even for a movie fan like me, the plot gets confusing. It's a daunting mission, and for all these reasons, this film could produce more arguments about whether it's a success or not than the previous film did.

The positives: John Williams gives us yet another fantastic musical score that brings all the right emotions to glorious visual scenes. Similarly, the technical department continues to amaze the audience, with gorgeous set designs, vivid cinematography and a striking combination of visual and practical effects. These guys know how to make things look good and sound good.

The negatives: the film's plot and storyline move quickly with a lot of ground to cover. This means some aspects are just not developed; there's no time to allow the viewer to understand the meaning of certain events and revelations.

A lot of the story depends on Kylo Ren and Rey. Adam Driver and Daisy Ridley put in excellent performances that are believable to the audience. The scenes with them together are always the most engaging. John Boyega and Oscar Isaac also get more time to build on the bromance with Finn and Poe, leading to some good laughs, and yet, there's not quite enough of them.

The original trilogy favourites Chewbacca, R2-D2, C-3PO and Lando Calrissian (Billy Dee Williams) get their moments, but we deserve to see more of them, and it feels like something is missing there. There are some intriguing new characters, but they don't do enough to matter eventually. Fortunately, the action scenes are immense and are always rewarding.

Certainly, the film wraps up the new trilogy, but in my opinion the storyline wasn't clearly outlined, and it shows.

HINT

Trilogy – a movie or book in three parts

Neat ending – a good conclusion to a movie

Ground to cover – a lot of the story to cover

Bromance – a combination of 'brother' and 'romance' to show a close friendship between men

HINT

Remember how to structure your paragraphs.

- Have one main topic sentence.
- Include two or three supporting sentences.
- Join sentences with connectives: like, first, then, finally, etc.
- Use a variety of sentences (different kinds and lengths).

3 Answer these questions in your notebook.

a Aside from the paragraph called 'The negatives', what other negative comments does Ms Walker have about the movie? Make a list.

b Aside from the paragraph called 'The positives', what other positive comments does Ms Walker have about the movie? Make a list.

c Write down three words which show that the scenery in the movie is excellent.

d Write down three phrases which show that the movie did not develop to its full potential, in the reviewer's opinion.

e In your opinion, does what the reviewer says about the movie match the 3.5 star rating?

Try this

Write a review of a movie you have seen recently. It does not have to be a sci-fi movie.

Use this writing frame to help you.

Title:	
Actors:	
Director:	
Star rating:	
Brief summary of what the movie is about:	
Your opinion of it:	
Why you recommend or don't recommend the movie:	

Speaking and listening

Is there life out there?

1 Do you believe that there is life elsewhere in the universe? Discuss this in your group.
- What is an interstellar object?
- What is a '**UFO**'?
- Discuss a good definition for the term 'extra-terrestrial life'.

2 Work with a partner. Listen to this discussion among friends about other possible life forms in the universe in Audio 7.3. As you listen, find answers to these questions.

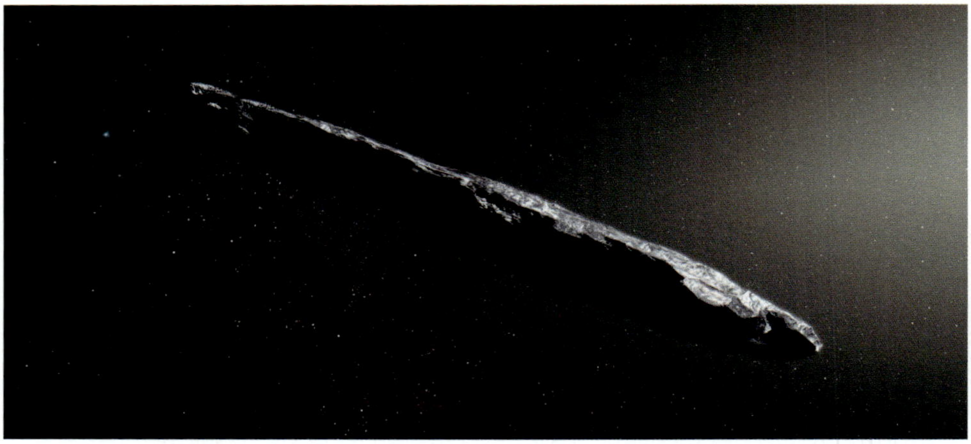

▲ Oumuamua, the first interstellar object that has travelled through our solar system

3 What is Bea's attitude when she says, 'So, is this a secret scientist meeting or something?'
- What is she implying about the boys?
- Does she feel included or left out? How can you tell?

4 Shalin answers her by quoting from a very respectable newspaper.
- What does this imply about what he believes about Oumuamua?
- How do you think he feels about Bea's sarcastic comment?

5 How does Miles show his support for Shalin?
- What examples does he give to show his support?

6 Why do you think Bea refuses to remember the name Oumuamua?
- What does this imply about her belief in extra-terrestrial life?

7 How does Bea join in with the boys?
- What thoughts does she offer to be part of their group?
- How does Shalin acknowledge that she is part of their group?

8 Miles says 'Is this a joke?'
- What does that imply about how he sees the 'ultimate story about people sighting UFOs'?

9 How does Bea build up the tension in the story?
   - Does she pause dramatically? Repeat words? Slow down her speech?

10 What do you think happened next?

DID YOU KNOW?

If you want to find out what happened next, you can Google the story. Look for 'Betty and Barney Hill'.

LET'S TALK

Look at the photograph of 'crop circles'. Some people believe that they are made by extra-terrestrials.

- What do you think?
- How else could these circles have been made?

CHALLENGE YOURSELF

Prepare a talk to give to the class. You are going to be telling a story about an encounter with a UFO/extra-terrestrial being. You can base your talk on research, or on your own or a family member's experience.

- Give your talk a title.
- Plan your talk, using a mind map.
- You need:
  - an introduction to begin your story
  - a descriptive account of what happened/who or what you encountered
  - a conclusion to the story
  - plus your own feelings or commentary about your experience.

Writing

Write about a space adventure

You are going to write a story about space travel. You have already chosen one of these topics, and begun to work on ideas.

- My journey to Mars
- Living on Mars

Try this

You have done a lot of preparation throughout this unit for your story. You've looked at how to breathe in a different atmosphere, growing or eating food, and ways of living and travelling. Now, it is time to put it all together into a story.

1 Plan your work. Start by making a mind map of your ideas. You can use this outline to help you.

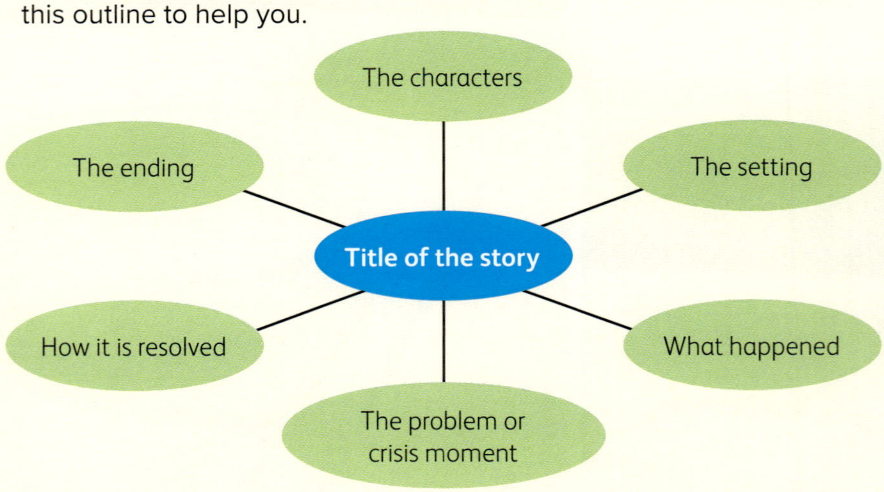

2 Now use your mind map to make a rough draft of your story. Remember these key points:

- Each paragraph should have one main topic sentence, which is then supported by two or three sentences. For example:

> This is it – blast off! The engines growled. The tension mounted. We were ready at last.

- Use connecting words to join your paragraphs into a coherent story. For example, next paragraph:

> Then, we were pushed back into our seats. My arms trembled. My mouth was dry, ...

- Next paragraph:

> Finally, we had lift-off. Immediately, we knew ...

- Vary the kinds of sentences you use. Think of exclamations, questions, longer sentences when someone is thinking. This gives your writing feeling and movement. For example:

> Would we ever get there? I wondered if it had all been a horrible mistake, and I had left behind everything I knew for nothing. No! This will work!

3 Swap your rough draft with a partner. Check each other's work.
- Check that you have structured your story correctly, according to the mind map. Does it have an introduction, a setting, good characters, an action point and a resolution?
- Does each paragraph have a strong topic sentence, with supporting sentences?
- Are paragraphs joined with connecting words?
- Check the spelling and punctuation.

4 Now edit and revise your story, after the useful feedback from your partner. Write out your story neatly, and then hand it in, with all your notes, to your teacher. You should hand in your
- mind map
- rough draft with your partner's markings on it
- final neat copy.

Now you have completed Unit 7, you may like to try the Unit 7 online knowledge test if you are using the Boost eBook.

Self check

In your story, have you used the new grammar of this unit? You should have
- used the past perfect active and passive forms
- used a range of past perfect continuous forms
- added useful and interesting detail to your essay by using relative clauses, which tell you more about people, places and things.

What can you do?

Read and review what you can do.
- I can listen to an argument about space exploration, to information about useful inventions that come from space travel and to a radio interview about extra-terrestrial life.
- I can talk about space travel, the possibility of life on other planets and tell the story of an encounter with a UFO.
- I can read about a space trip to Mars and a film review of a sci-fi film.
- I can write a story about a voyage to Mars or about living on Mars, and a film review.
- I can use a range of active and passive past perfect simple forms, past perfect continuous forms and relative clauses, including 'which' to refer to the previous clause.

8 Rules protect us ... don't they?

In this unit you will:

- listen to a talk about rules and a discussion about old and new school rules
- give views about the value of rules for keeping us safe
- read articles about different reasons for breaking rules
- write an article about rules for keeping us safe
- use simple past and present continuous tenses
- use a range of connectives when speaking and writing.

Speaking and listening

Breaking the rules

1 Work in groups. Look at pictures on the opposite page and discuss the following questions.
- Which pictures show people breaking a rule?
- What rule are they breaking?

DID YOU KNOW?

A rule or a **regulation** is something that tells you what you may or may not do. There are school rules and rules for different games/sports, for example.

A law is a rule made by a country or part of a country which tells you what you can or cannot do. The law of a country is the set of laws by which a country is ruled or governed.

If you break the rules or laws (do not obey rules and laws), you may be punished in some way.

2 Listen to Audio 8.1 about breaking rules and laws.

3 What are the main ideas of this audio? Select statements from the list below.

a Laws and rules are made to protect us and help us behave correctly.
b The rules about driving, walking and cycling are designed to keep us safe.
c 'No **trespassing**' signs keep people out of certain areas.
d It is not against the law to damage public property.
e Special rules are sometimes made during emergency situations.
f Social distancing is now law in most countries.

PRACTISE

Work in pairs. Tell your partner why you think there are rules in school, at home and in countries. You should also say what would happen if these did not exist.

Try this

Work in groups. Look again at the pictures on the opposite page that show people breaking a rule.
- Why are these people breaking a rule? Because they think the law is wrong? Because they don't know about the law or rule? Because they like breaking rules and laws?
- Will they be punished for this? How? Will they get a fine?
- What do you think should happen to these people? Why? Give a reason and use 'because' in your answer.

Speaking and listening

Old rules, new rules

1 School and college rules have changed over time. Look at the picture below which shows how much money students would be fined for disobeying certain rules at an old university in the UK.
Work in pairs.

- **a** Make a list of what you think the rules were. You can use modern English and words you know!
- **b** Look up words (such as **lobby** and **quadrangle**) if you are not sure what they mean.
- **c** Compare your rules with others in the class.
- **d** What do you think of these rules? Do you have rules like this at your school? Should lyou have rules like these?

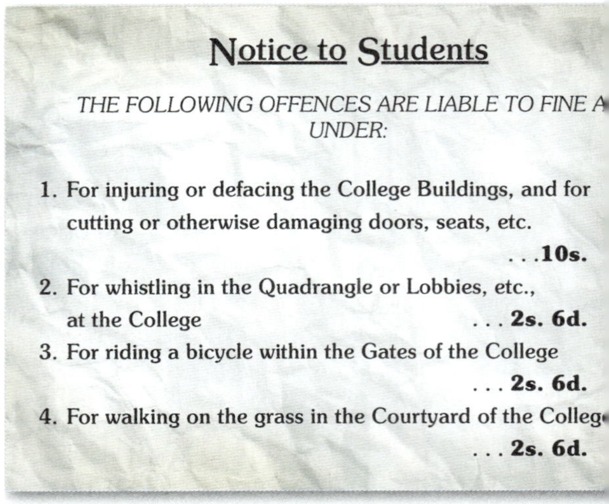

Notice to Students

THE FOLLOWING OFFENCES ARE LIABLE TO FINE A[S] UNDER:

1. For injuring or defacing the College Buildings, and for cutting or otherwise damaging doors, seats, etc. . . .**10s.**
2. For whistling in the Quadrangle or Lobbies, etc., at the College . . . **2s. 6d.**
3. For riding a bicycle within the Gates of the College . . . **2s. 6d.**
4. For walking on the grass in the Courtyard of the Colleg[e] . . . **2s. 6d.**

2 Listen to Audio 8.2, a conversation between father and son. The father is telling his son about the rules they had when he was at school many years before.

3 Complete this summary of the main ideas of the audio you listened to.

> A father and son discussed how school rules (had changed/has worn). The father thinks that the school uniforms or clothes today are (more/less) comfortable than in his day. The father wore (a **blazer** and tie/a hoodie and tie) to school. The father had special clothes for sports and (so does the son/but the son does not). The father was not (encouraged/allowed) to discuss things in class. As a punishment, the father had to write (lines/laws) a thousand times. The father thought this (was/was not) a good punishment. The son thinks the rules at his school are (too strict/not strict enough).

HINT

Make sure you can give reasons for your answers. For example:

We think the rule about running is a good idea because it's easy to slip and hurt yourself if you run inside the buildings.

PRACTISE

Work in groups. Read the school rules on the conversation cards that your teacher will give you. Choose five rules and discuss them in your group.

- Do you have a rule like this at your school?
- Does the rule aim to protect you or control your behaviour?
- What is your opinion of the rule?
- How could you change the rule to make it more appropriate for your school?

Share and discuss your ideas with the class afterwards.

Try this

Work in groups. You are going to set up a new social group using social media that is available to you. It has been suggested that you should introduce some rules to make sure the group is protected and that it works the way you want it to work.

1 Make a draft list of five rules for your social group. Here are some examples:
   - The person who sets up the group can decide who becomes part of the group.
   - Don't post photographs and comments more than twice a day.
   - Don't like your own posts.
   - Don't share posts with people outside the group.
   - Be supportive, kind and mindful of the feelings of others when posting comments.

2 Discuss your draft rules with another group in the class.
   - Is it a good idea to have some rules? Why,t or why not?
   - Will the rules work?
   - How will you enforce the rules?

CHALLENGE YOURSELF

Do you think a school can work without school rules?

Write down your opinion and give a reason for your answer.

Use of English

Talking about the past

Do you remember?

We use the simple past tense to describe completed actions. We can use the active or the passive voice in the past tense. For example:

The school did not allow us to wear joggers. (active)

We were not allowed to wear joggers. (passive)

PRACTISE

Work in pairs. Explain to your partner how to form the simple past tense in the active and the passive.

- In the active, add ________ to the verb stem, if the verb is regular.
- Check if the verb is irregular, check the form in a dictionary (or on page 159.)
- In the passive, use the verb ________ + the ________ participle of the verb.

The words 'used to' can be used in different ways and they have different meanings. Look at the following examples:

I used to wear a blazer at school.

(This describes a repeated action in the past which has now changed.)

I am used to wearing a blazer to school.

(This describes something you are familiar with in the present.)

I can't/couldn't get used to wearing a blazer.

(This describes an action in the present or the past that you cannot or could not become familiar with or accustomed to.)

PRACTISE

Work in pairs. Put the following sentences in the simple past tense. Use the verb given in brackets. Then, say if each sentence is active or passive.

1 I (to have) to stand up and greet the teacher.
2 We (to use) wear blazers.
3 I (not to allow) to wear shorts to school.
4 We (not to encourage) to discuss things.
5 You (to wear) a cap and a tie when you were at school?
6 My dad (to have to stand up) when a teacher walked into the classroom.
7 My mum says that she had to wear tights when she (to be) at school.
8 We (can) not run inside the school buildings when we (to be) at school.

Try this

1 What do you wear to school? Do you have a uniform? Look at these photographs. Then imagine what you would say about your school 'uniform' if you are talking about it in 20 years' time.
Write ten sentences to describe what you wore. Remember to use the simple past tense.

2 Still imagining you are talking 20 years in the future, write down five rules that you had to obey at school. Say why you think each rule was important or not important in your view. You can do this in a table, like this:

	Rule	What I thought about the rule
1	We had to be at school on time.	I think this was important because we had to start work as a class. If people were late, we had to repeat things or they missed important information.
2		
3		
4		
5		

CHALLENGE YOURSELF

Interview your parents or other adults in your family about the rules they had to obey when they went to school. Write a paragraph about this in the simple past tense.

Then, read your paragraph aloud to the class. As you read, emphasise different words and use a different tone of voice to show how you feel about the information.

HINT

Mark the words in the paragraph that you want to emphasise. For example:

My mum <u>had</u> to wear <u>tights</u> when she was at school!!!!

Reading

Rethinking the rules

Some people break rules in order to protest about something or because they think a rule or law is wrong. Others break the rules for enjoyment, in order to make money or to get something they want.

1 Look at the photographs and read the headlines and the captions. Do not read the articles yet. Say what you think these articles are about.

2 Do you know what these words mean? Match the words and their meanings before you read the articles.

exploit	Something that is against the law
endangered	To use something in a bad way, either to get something you want or to make money
illegal	Respected
honoured	In danger of disappearing (animals and plants)

3 Read the articles in detail.

WILL PANGOLINS BE SAVED?

Pangolins have been exploited for years and, as a result, many of the species are now endangered. Despite laws which are designed to protect them, thousands of pangolins in Africa and Asia are still being caught and killed. They are sold as meat and their **scales** are sold for making traditional medicines. But things are changing. New laws are being made to protect these animals further. In China, for example, the government has removed pangolin scales from a list of approved ingredients in traditional medicine. This means that the scales cannot be used in traditional medicines. Is this going to stop the illegal trade in these animals? It is going to make a difference …

▲ The bodies of pangolins are covered in flat, hard scales. In 2019, more than 97 tons of these scales from 150,000 pangolins were intercepted by customs authorities in different countries

ROOF-TOPPING RULE-BREAKERS

The building-owners don't like it, but jumping between city high rises and leaping across ledges are favourite stunts for extreme parkour groups. Of course, parkour can be very dangerous, and it takes years of dedicated training for these athletes to master specialist extreme parkour skills. But what rules are they breaking? Well, according to the building owners, the roof-toppers are trespassing. They also risk damaging the buildings or injuring themselves, and they are taking videos of the buildings without permission. Even though it is not illegal, the building owners say that parkour should be banned in urban areas.

The roof-toppers see it differently, of course. They argue that they are not hurting anyone, defacing any property or breaking any laws, and point out that their millions of followers love tuning in to watch them on YouTube. They say that they are exercising outdoors in the fresh air, challenging themselves and keeping fit, hanging out with their friends, and most importantly, they are having fun. 'Anyway,' they say, 'no one would be able to catch us!'

▲ The extreme sport of parkour

LET'S TALK

Work in pairs or small groups and talk about the articles you have read. Discuss and answer these questions.

Text: Will pangolins be saved?

- What laws about pangolins have been broken?
- Why did they break the law?
- What is being done about this now?

Text: Roof-topping rule-breakers

- What laws are the extreme parkour athletes breaking?
- Why do the building owners want extreme parkour banned?
- What do you think? Should these parkour athletes be punished?

Which text did you find more interesting? Why?

CHALLENGE YOURSELF

Work in pairs and do some research on an animal that is trafficked (captured and sold illegally).

You could choose pangolins or animals such as rhinos, elephants or chimpanzees.

- Find out how and why people break the law to traffic these animals.
- Find out what effects this has had.
- Write notes and do a short presentation to the class about what you have found out.

Use of English

Present continuous verb forms

Do you remember?

We use the present continuous tense

- to say what is happening at the moment, as we are speaking

I am wearing my school uniform today.

- to talk about future arrangements.

I am finding out more about the trade in pangolins tomorrow.

Do you remember how to form this tense?

We use the passive form of the present continuous tense in a similar way. We use the passive:

- when we don't need to say who does the action
- if we don't want to say who the subject is.

For example:

	Active voice	Passive voice
Present continuous	The parkour athletes are climbing high-rise buildings. People are still catching thousands of pangolins in Africa and Asia. Why are they hunting pangolins?	High-rise buildings are being climbed by parkour athletes. Thousands of pangolins in Africa and Asia are still being caught. Why are pangolins being hunted?

Study the examples above and explain to your partner how to form the present continuous passive form.

PRACTISE

Work in pairs. Make sentences and questions in the present continuous tense. Use the given words and add your own words if necessary. You can make sentences in the active or the passive voice.

1 to make/traditional medicine/with pangolin scales
2 to wear/school uniforms/this school/students
3 roof runners/dangerous stunts to practise
4 why/parkour athletes/buildings/videos/to take?
5 how/to stop/building owners/parkour athletes/?

Do you remember?

You have learned to use connectives in many different ways. For example:

- to link words, clauses, sentences and ideas
- to help to put events in sequence
- to give explanations, examples, reasons and purpose
- to contrast or show the difference between ideas.

Here are a few examples:

There are speed limits on roads, so that we do not drive too fast.

While/although public marches are often allowed, you may need permission to do this.

The parkour athletes climbed the building and after that they jumped onto the next roof.

Try this

Which sentence in each pair is grammatically correct? Write the correct sentences in your notebook.

1. a School rules are change so that we have more freedom to decide what we wear to school.
   b School rules are changing so that we have more freedom to decide what we wear to school.
2. a The trespass rules are being ignored by the roof-toppers.
   b The trespass rules are being ignore by the roof-toppers.
3. a The parkour athletes are being asked to go home.
   b The parkour athletes are been asked to go home.
4. a Pangolin scales are not being using in traditional medicine any more.
   b Pangolin scales are not being used in traditional medicine any more.

Connectives

Do you know these connectives? Look at the way they are used.

There are laws. Thousands of pangolins are still being caught and killed.

Despite laws, thousands of pangolins are still being caught and killed.

I believe that school rules are quite important. My friends do not believe this.

Unlike my friends, I believe that school rules are quite important.

PRACTISE

Work in pairs and discuss how to join the sentences with the connectives given in brackets. Write your answers in your notebook and share them with the class.

1. I think that school uniforms are silly. My parents do not agree. (unlike)
2. She doesn't think people should be fined for roof-topping. Her brother thinks people should be fined for roof-topping. (unlike)
3. The weather was bad. Many parkour athletes arrived. (despite)
4. The school rules say we may not wear jewellery to school. My friend always wears jewellery. (despite)

CHALLENGE YOURSELF

Look at the sentences you wrote in the Practise exercise on page 130. Can you think of other ways of joining the clauses, using different connectives? Rewrite the sentences with different connectives. You will need to change the sentences a little.

Reading

Breaking rules by mistake

1 Before you read, discuss what you think a neighbourhood charter is.
2 Read this article silently. As you read, make a note of any words you do not understand.
3 Then read the text again and try and work out the meanings from the context.

The rules you may not even know exist!

Have you ever broken a rule by mistake, maybe even a rule you didn't know existed, and had to pay the consequences? Did you think this was unfair?

We know that rules are usually made to help and protect us, so we know how to behave and know what to expect of others. However, not all rules are quite so straightforward. Certain rules make perfect sense, and we can decode them with no problems at all, while others are open to interpretation – or even misinterpretation.

This is certainly the situation when you are travelling in other countries and you don't understand how to validate your train or bus ticket. Or, even more simply, if you move to a new school and haven't yet learned the school rules. For example, you might think it's perfectly reasonable to use your phone to check how to spell a word, not realising that phones are banned in class. You might not expect your new teacher to be quite so angry to see you with a phone in your hand ... I mean, how do you know what you don't know, right? OK, fair enough, you will learn the new set of school rules because you definitely don't want to make the same mistake again. There's nothing for it but just to accept the rule without questioning it.

But what if you are travelling in another country and you cannot speak or read much of the language of that country? Or what if the rules have not been clearly displayed? How are you supposed to know not to stand in a particular place on the train platform if the rule is only written on a tiny sign half hidden behind a bin, for instance? There are people who receive hefty fines for things they don't even know are against the rules, like accidentally dropping litter or chewing gum on public transport in some countries.

Closer to home, it's worth knowing what your local rules are so that you don't inadvertently break them. Here, I am talking about what kind of behaviour is acceptable in your country, town or neighbourhood. There may even be a 'neighbourhood charter' outlining what seemingly innocent acts are actually against the rules where you live. Look below at some of the rules in a neighbourhood charter which was drawn up for a suburb in Australia.

- Do not use a neighbour's unsecure Wi-Fi connection without their consent.
- Only cut back your neighbour's tree branches as far as they overhang your land. Cutting back any further is not allowed.
- If you take fruit from a neighbour's tree – even if it overhangs onto your land – it can be seen as stealing. It's polite to ask first!
- Smoke, whether from a wood burner in the house or a barbecue in the garden, can be a nuisance. Check with your neighbours before you light a fire.
- When positioning a trampoline, be mindful of its placement to avoid children being able to see into other people's gardens and violating their privacy. Also, make sure they don't make too much noise.
- Bright security lighting, if shining directly into a neighbour's property, can constitute light pollution.

> **DID YOU KNOW?**
> A charter is a legal document which guarantees certain rights. One of the most famous and oldest charters is the Magna Carta, which was created in England in 1215 and signed by King John. The Magna Carta is Latin for 'The Great Charter' and it contains over 60 clauses, covering many areas of the nation's life, including the right to a fair trial.

▲ A painting showing King John signing the Magna Carta

4 Do you think having a neighbourhood charter is a good idea? Why, or why not?
5 Imagine you have been asked to write a neighbourhood charter for the area where you live. What rules would you include? Would there be punishments for people who broke the rules? Why, or why not?

Vocabulary

1 What do the prefixes in each of these words mean?

disobey	misinterpretation	decode
unusual	inadvertently	illegal

2 Use the prefixes above to make words with the opposite meaning.
- a understand
- b correct
- c exploited
- d respect
- e comfortable
- f forest
- g legitimate

3 Choose four words that you have made and make your own sentences with the words.

Read the text again. Write your answers to these questions in your notebook.

4 What should you not use in class?
5 State two things you should not do when travelling in another country.
6 State two things you should not do in the Australian neighbourhood described in the text.

Try this

1 What is the overall tone of the writer in the text?
2 Work in pairs and discuss the implied meanings in each of these sentences from the text you read. Use the questions to guide you.
   - a Or even misinterpretation.
     - Is the writer encouraging us to break rules?
   - b There's nothing for it but just to accept the rule without questioning it.
     - Is the writer telling us to always follow rules?
   - c There may even be a 'neighbourhood charter' outlining what seemingly innocent acts are actually against the rules where you live.
     - Is the writer annoyed?
     - Is the writer saying that all neighbourhoods have rules and that we all know about them?

LET'S TALK

Work in groups and discuss the questions posed in the last paragraph of the text that you read.

1 Which of these rules do you think it would be easy to break if you didn't know they existed?
2 Do you think people who break these kinds of rules by mistake should be punished?
3 What do you think should happen to them, and why?

Try this

1 Look at the image below and discuss what it means.
2 Some rules in society are not written down. They are etiquette rules for how to behave or act properly. For example, in some countries you should not eat in a public place or put your bag on an empty seat next to you on a train if the train is crowded. Can you share three rules which a tourist coming to your country should know?

Speaking and listening

Thrill seekers extreme?

1 Listen to Audio 8.3, a young photographer talking about his interest in urban exploring. Make notes on the main ideas.

2 Then work with a partner and compare notes. Discuss and agree what the main ideas are. Listen to the audio again to confirm your ideas.

Now read this summary before you attempt the Let's Talk activity below.

Parkour athletes who break the rules may be banned from playing their sport. They lose their income and may lose their **reputation** as well. Urban explorers may also be fined for accessing buildings without permission. Some people break other kinds of rules like speeding or using their mobile phones while driving. Sometimes these drivers are fined or banned from driving, although in some countries they are offered driver improvement courses instead. Some people think that drivers who break the rules should be helped to drive better rather than being prevented from driving.

Try this

As you listen to the arguments during the debate, make summary notes about the main ideas. Listen to the arguments and the reasons given to support the arguments. You can use these in the article you are going to write next.

LET'S TALK

Have a class debate about the value of school rules or rules in society in general. You should speak for or against the following statement:

Rules are made to keep us safe.

- Work in groups and discuss the statement above.
- Then, decide if you will speak for or against the topic.
- Choose two speakers from your group to represent your group. Help each speaker to develop a short argument. Each speaker should give two good reasons for why they are speaking for or against the topic.
- After each speaker has presented their argument, you will have time to discuss the arguments as a class.
- Each speaker will then sum up the main ideas again at the end of the debate.

HINT

- Always give examples when you give reasons, as this helps people to understand what you mean. For example:

Rules keep us safe and help us do the right thing, whether the rules are driving laws or school rules about wearing the correct uniform. Sometimes we need to be reminded of this. I heard of someone who was caught by the police for speeding. After having been told of the risks at a speed awareness course, she now always drives within the speed limit.

- Use connectives in your arguments. For example:

Unlike being banned from driving, which can have a negative impact on someone's life, alternative measures can help people improve their behaviour. Therefore, they are not likely to speed again or use their phone while driving in future.

Writing

Write a short article

You have debated about the value of rules keeping us safe and now you are going to write a short article about this on the topic: 'Rules are made to keep us safe'.

Before you begin to plan your article, work in pairs and discuss the value of rules designed to keep us safe on the road. Discuss the road signs below.

- What is the speed limit for driving in the city in your country?
- Why do we have road signs?
- Do you think they are effective?

Try this

Your article should be about 200–250 words.

1 Start with the summary you made during the debate. Which arguments do you think are the most important or interesting? Choose two or three arguments and write them down. You could use a mind map.

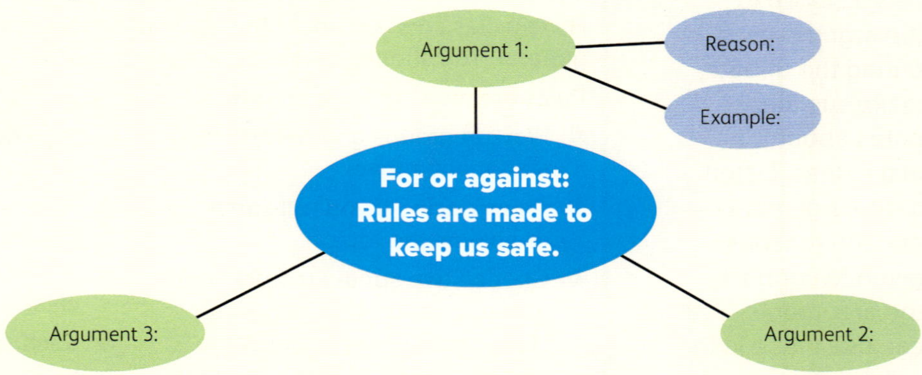

2 Think about how you will convince your reader about each argument.
- What reason will you give to support each argument?
- What examples will you give?

Add these to your plan.

3 Now think of a good opening statement that will make people want to read your article. Here are some examples you could use or adapt:

Banning someone from driving is not an effective measure to reduce speeding on our roads.

Education is much more effective than punishment.

If people understand the reasons for rules, they are much more likely to follow them.

4 Now use your completed plan to write a rough draft of your article. Remember!
- Each paragraph should have one main topic sentence (your argument), which is then supported by two or three sentences (your reasons and examples to support the argument).
- Use connecting words to join your paragraphs into a coherent argument.
- Use the present continuous tense in the active or passive voice to refer to current events.

For example:

We are more likely to follow rules if we understand why rules have been made. Some people's lives are being put at risk when others unnecessarily drive too fast in cities. Therefore, we should educate all drivers that speed limits are made for a reason.

5 Swap your rough draft with a partner. Check each other's work and give each other feedback. Discuss what a suitable headline would be for each article.

6 Finally, write your article neatly.

HINT

Headlines do not have to be complete sentences and it is better if they are short. Choose key verbs and nouns carefully to attract the attention of your reader. For example:

Raise awareness – don't ban!

Self check

In your article
- Have you built up an argument, giving reasons for your statements?
- Have you used some new connectives to link sentences and ideas?
- Have you used some passive forms in the present continuous and past tenses?

What can you do?

Read and review what you can do.
- I can talk about rules and discuss old and new school rules.
- I can listen to a speech about staying safe while exploring abandoned places.
- I can give my views about the value of rules for keeping us safe.
- I can read articles about different reasons for making laws to protect us.
- I can write an article about the value of rules for keeping us safe.
- I can use simple past and present continuous tenses.
- I can use a range of connectives when speaking and writing.

Now you have completed Unit 8, you may like to try the Unit 8 online knowledge test if you are using the Boost eBook.

9 Dreams and ambitions

In this unit you will:

- listen to a discussion among friends, an interview with a psychologist about how to achieve your dreams and a young person discussing their dream board
- talk about your dreams and ambitions for the future
- read about famous people who have achieved their dreams
- write a letter to your future self and a poem about your dreams
- use a range of past continuous active and passive forms, a range of abstract nouns, compound nouns and complex noun phrases, and a wide range of pronouns.

▲ You could be a famous basketball player, like Michael Jordan

▲ Or an astronaut who travels into outer space

▲ Perhaps you'll write a best-selling novel

▲ Or maybe you'll make movies

Speaking and listening

> **HINT**
> You do not have to reveal anything personal, if you wish to keep your goals private. Use the photographs on the opposite page to make up sentences in your group.

Do you have a dream?

1 In your group, talk about your dreams and ambitions for the future.
- Do you have a long-term dream for the future? For example: 'I would like to travel around South East Asia on a bicycle', 'I would like to study to be a beautician' or 'I'd like to study astrophysics'. Share your goals with your group.
- What about short-term goals? For example: 'I want to get on the first cricket team', 'I'm saving to buy a drum kit' or 'I'm planning a camping trip at the end of the year with friends'.

2 Our friends Massimo, Priti, Aoife and Kofi are back. Listen to Audio 9.1 where they are talking about their plans for the future.

3 Talk about these questions in your group.

a What is Priti's opinion of Massimo's food?

b What is Massimo implying when he says to Aoife, 'Are you going to leave us all behind?'

c What does 'Star of stage and screen' imply?

d Why is Aoife offended by Kofi saying 'I have to do something more **meaningful**'?

e What is Massimo's opinion of Kofi's ambitions?

PRACTISE

Work in groups of four. You are going to read the text together. You discussed the opinions and the implied meanings in the last exercise. Now see if you can emphasise these with your voices. Think about what each person says. Are they making a joke? Is Aoife really offended by Kofi? How does Priti sound when she's teasing Massimo about his food?

1 Identify what tone is required for each sentence and mark this on the worksheet your teacher gives you.

2 Underline the words that should be emphasised in each sentence, based on the tone you have assigned to that sentence.

3 Read the text aloud together and listen for words that show opinion.

4 Then listen to the audio again and check your pronunciation and intonation.

Speaking and listening

Listen to a motivational speaker

1 Listen to Audio 9.2, an interview with a psychologist about how to achieve your dreams. Make a mind map like this one in your notebook, to summarise the main points of her speech. As you listen, add more information to each bubble of the mind map.

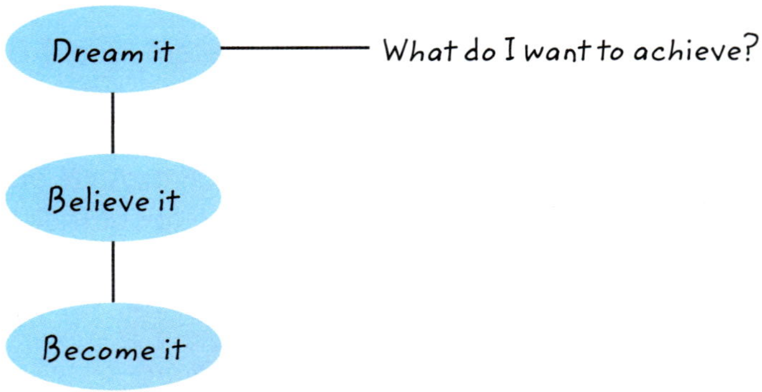

2 Work in your groups. Talk about the interview with the psychologist, Doctor X.

- Do you agree with the three stages she lays out?
- How would you separate fact from opinion here? It's not that easy to do.
- Would you agree that the facts are the people's lives and life experiences? Why, or why not?
- Is this whole interview based on opinion? What do you think?

DID YOU KNOW?

Oprah Winfrey is probably one of the most well-known motivational speakers in the world. She had her own TV show, then her own TV network. She also has a number of schools around the world that focus on education for girls.

Working the dream

PRACTISE

1 Talk about the work that people you admire have put into achieving their dreams. Use the past continuous tenses in your discussion. For example:

I admire Michael Jordan. He had been playing basketball for years before he was discovered.

I think Rhianna is fantastic. She has been using her music to raise money for the less fortunate through the foundation she set up in 2012.

Taylor Swift has been doing some interesting work recently. She has been moving away from just music, and is becoming a social activist too.

2 Who else do you admire, who has achieved their dream through hard work and dedication?

- a Discuss this in class. One person acts as a scribe and writes the names of the people on the board. He or she should separate the names into categories – sportspeople, actors, adventurers, social activists, etc.
- b Get into groups, based on these different categories.
- c Discuss the selection of people in your group. What is common about the way they each reached their dream? Is there a pattern?
- d Make short notes about what is similar in their journeys, and what is different.
- e Prepare to report back to the class on what you have found out.

Try this

Not everyone knows what they want to do in the future. Making a dream board, where you pin ideas and thoughts, can be very useful. You are going to be building a dream board throughout this unit. You can do this on a piece of poster paper, with cut-out pictures and pieces of text, or you can use software such as Pinterest to collect pictures.

1 Start now by discussing these questions in your group.
- What quotes or pieces of writing do you find inspirational?
- Are there people you admire? Are they movies stars, or entrepreneurs, sports stars, or influencers?
- What about song lyrics, or quotes from movies? What about cartoons, memes, jokes?
- Are there physical things that you touch that inspire you, like a soft velvety piece of cloth or a beaten-up piece of wood? What could you make with these items?

2 Think about all the things you could add to a dream board, and start collecting now.

HINT

Can your class get to a shared outcome on 'the route to achieving your dreams'? Are there things that are the same about how everyone becomes successful, regardless of what they do?

Use of English

Using the language of dreams

Let's talk about dreams. How many 'dream' words do you know?

PRACTISE

1 Work with a partner. Make sentences with these dependent prepositions, to show that you know what they mean. Then write your sentences in your notebook.

a dream on
b dream up
c dream about
d dream of

2 Make compound nouns with these dream words. Join as many words in the dream bubble as you can to make new words.

dream **day** catcher
boat **night** **mare,**
time **land**

Write the words in your notebook.

3 Use each of your new words in a sentence to show that you understand what they mean. Write your sentences into your notebook.

4 Answer these questions.

a What would you like to do, in your wildest dreams?
b What would be a dream come true, for you?
c What do you daydream about?
d What would your dream job be?
e Have you ever had a dream come true? What was it?

5 You know that 'dream' is an abstract noun, like 'love', 'happiness' and 'success'. Choose abstract nouns from the box to complete these sentences.

promise	anxiety	beauty	loyalty	love	determination

a He made it into the top three through sheer __________.
b It was her __________ for her grandmother that made her choose cooking as a career.
c The thought of sitting for exams gives me __________.
d They had made a __________ to their parents that they would start a trust fund in their name.
e Everyone admired the absolute __________ of the movie star.
f She stuck to the course out of __________ to her brother, who wanted her to succeed.

Do you remember?

Demonstrative pronouns point out a specific person or thing, or contact between people and things. Examples: *this*, *that*, *these* and *those*.

Indefinite pronouns refer to people in a general way. Examples: *some*, *one*, *anyone*, *someone*, *everyone*, *no one*.

Quantitative pronouns indicate an indefinite quantity. Examples: *some*, *any*, *none*, *much*, *many*, *little*, *few*.

Dreaming on

PRACTISE

1 Choose a demonstrative pronoun from the box to complete these sentences.

this that these those

a The problem is ________; I have no idea what I want to do after school.
b Dancing, art, publishing: ________ are all options you could choose.
c ________ is not going to help me solve my problem, as I prefer science or maths to arty things.
d ________ is your answer then; you need to study science or maths.
e I don't know how you always manage to do ________.
f Do what? I just offer advice, ________ is all I do.

2 Write the paragraph below into your notebook. Underline all the indefinite pronouns.

Not everyone is lucky enough to have a clear vision of what they want to do. Some have a vague outline – something in the arts, perhaps. Others have no clue at all. It is very helpful to go to a guidance counsellor, or to speak to someone in your family that you respect. You can only wait and hope for inspiration. And remember, dreaming is free; anyone can do it!

3 Use quantitative pronouns from the box to complete these sentences.

something all everyone everything many little few none anything nothing

a That is ________ I can do to help.
b You have to try ________ once!
c 'I need to do ________ more meaningful,' Kofi said.
d 'There are so ________, with so ________, that I need to do ________ to help.'
e 'Has there been news?' 'No, I haven't heard ________ yet.'
f ________ people understand that I want to be the mother of a large family. ________ thinks that's not an ambition, but for me it is.

Try this

Punctuate and correct this note from one friend to another, congratulating her on achieving her dream. Write out the correct note in full in your notebook.

> Deer Priti
>
> you now righting isn't my strong point but I have to let u now that im so proud of you!! Well done on getting into uni!!!
>
> I know you dream is acsually to have a huge familie but you can do that two after you qulify
>
> Lets get together and celebrate at mi plaice later
>
> Love and huggssss
>
> Aoife

Reading

Read about becoming famous

1 Becoming famous – is it luck or hard work? Discuss this in your group. Which of these is the most important? Rate these in importance, from 1 = most important to 4 = least important.

- Believing you can do it
- Hard work
- Visualising you can do it
- Good luck

Do the other members of your group agree with your rating?

2 You are going to read about two people who became famous. There are some areas in each of these pieces of writing where things are not clear. See if you can answer the questions in the text bubbles as you read.

Jim Carrey was a struggling stand-up comedian, who read too many self-help books. He had a job, but he also had bigger dreams. He would **visualise** things coming to him. As he said in an interview with Oprah Winfrey, 'I had nothing at that time, but visualising made me feel better. I would think to myself, "I do have these things but I just don't have my hands on them yet."'

Jim wrote himself a cheque for ten million dollars for 'acting services **rendered**' and dated it for five years' in the future. He put the cheque in his wallet, where it deteriorated and deteriorated. Then, just before the five years was up, he got offered the part in the movie *Dumb and Dumber*, for $10 million. Here's a brief clip of the discussion between Jim and Oprah.

Oprah: Visualisation works if you just work hard.

Jim: Yes, of course you have to work hard. You can't just visualise and then just go eat a sandwich.

Later, Oprah said: 'I loved that, that was such a powerful statement'.

What is missing here? Maybe a description of his dreams? How would you fix this?

And then? What happened? How did he feel?

Is this a reasonable argument? Do you think he just sat around 'visualising'?

Something's missing here too. What would you add for this to connect to the rest of the writing?

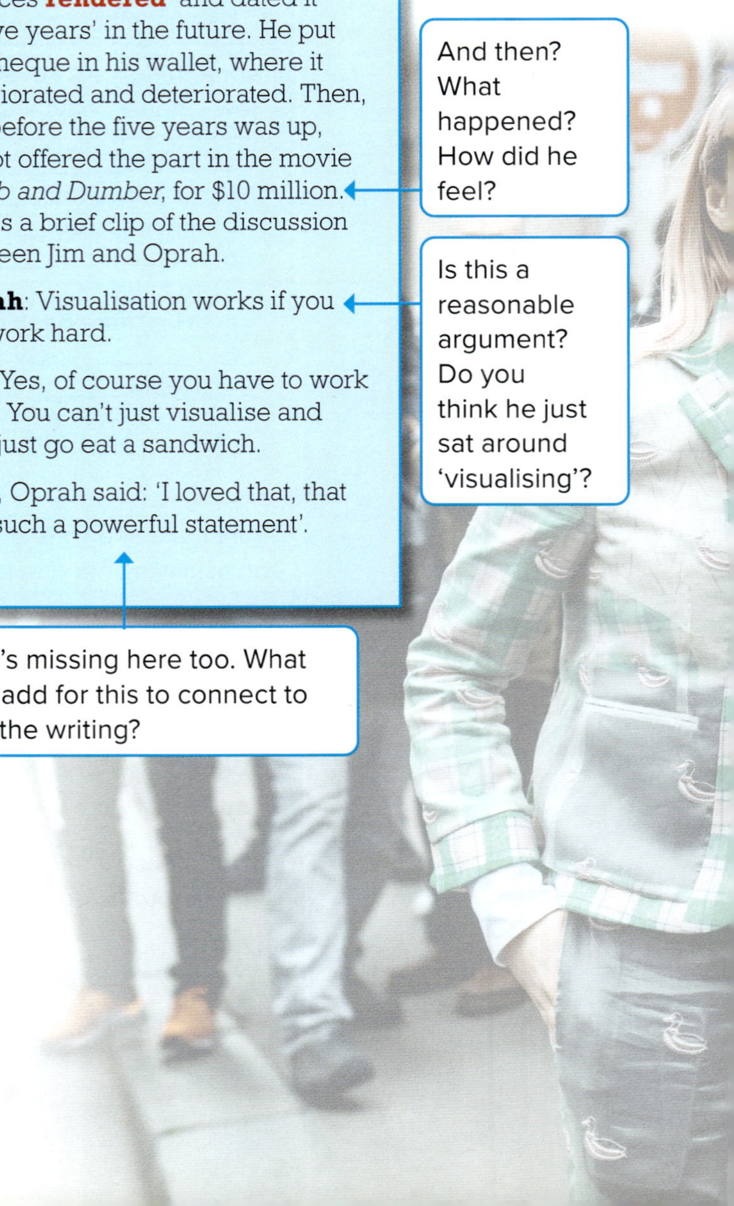

Maisie Williams was only eleven when she landed a part in *Game of Thrones*.

She went to an ordinary school, and got ordinary grades, and was ordinary at everything – except for how she felt on the inside. She had big dreams of becoming a professional dancer.

Remember this point. At the end come back to this.

At eight years old, she enrolled in dance class, and then at ten she decided she wanted to go to stage school like 'Billy Elliot'. Two successful **auditions** followed, but the family was unable to raise the funding which would allow Maisie to attend the stage school. It was, perhaps, a blessing in disguise, she said later.

What is a 'blessing in disguise'? Why was Maisie not upset about this, when she looked back at her experiences?

At the age of eleven, her dance teacher entered her into a talent show. She met Louise, who was delighted by her, and asked her to join her acting agency. Maisie worried that the 30 hours a week she spent dancing would suffer. What if she auditioned and didn't get a part? What would happen then?

There was no need to worry. In February, Maisie went to an audition in the local Methodist church for a part in a series called *Game of Thrones*. As she describes it, she harnessed all her insecurities, and self-doubt, and in the interview, she was 'cheeky, loud and angry' and just perfect for the part.

After getting the part and filming the pilot, the show grew to become one of the biggest shows in TV history. It has received 130 Emmy nominations, an eighth season, and has run for almost a decade.

Maisie grew from a child to adult during the eight seasons. What has she learned, that she can pass on to us? 'Don't strive to be famous, strive to be talented.'

What happened to her dream? What was her original dream?

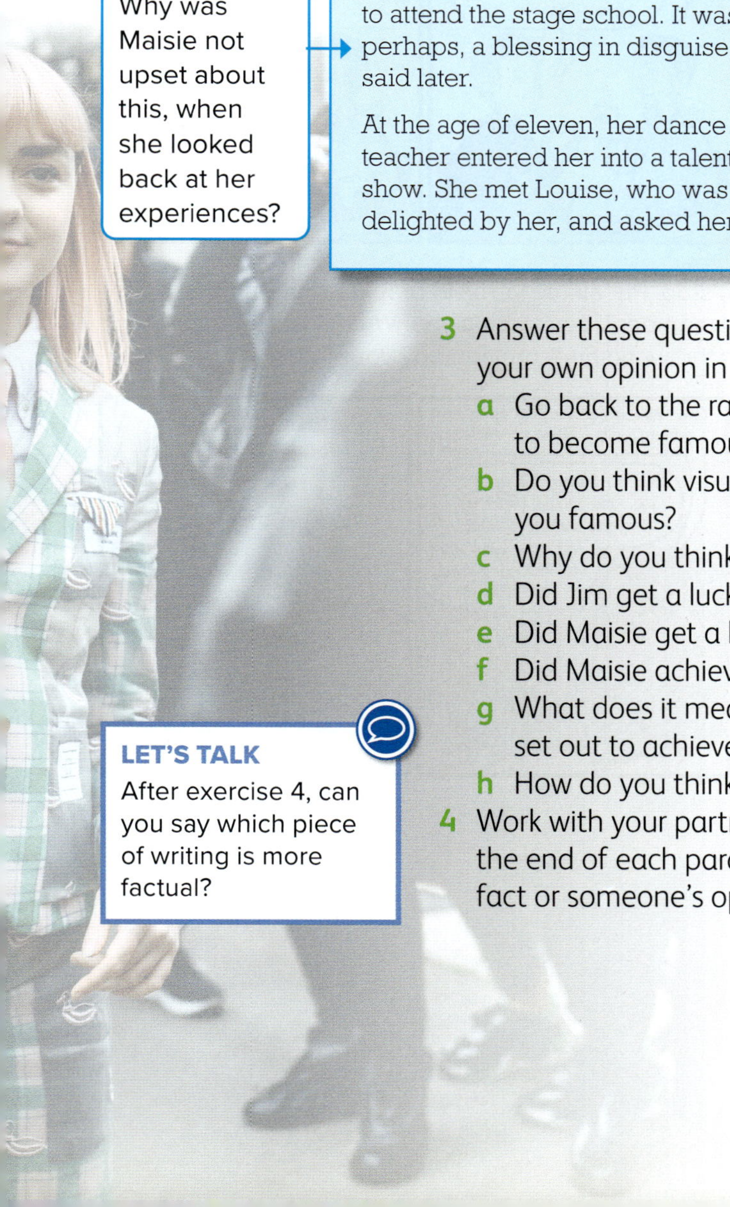

3 Answer these questions. Talk about them with a partner, but then write your own opinion in your notebook.

- a Go back to the ratings in exercise 1. What did Jim and Maisie both do to become famous?
- b Do you think visualising yourself as a famous person can make you famous?
- c Why do you think writing himself a cheque helped Jim?
- d Did Jim get a lucky break, or was it his hard work paying off?
- e Did Maisie get a lucky break, or was it her hard work paying off?
- f Did Maisie achieve her dream?
- g What does it mean if you achieve a different dream from the one you set out to achieve?
- h How do you think Maisie feels about becoming famous?

4 Work with your partner. Read through the texts again together. Stop at the end of each paragraph and, for each sentence, discuss whether it is a fact or someone's opinion.

LET'S TALK

After exercise 4, can you say which piece of writing is more factual?

Use of English

Talking about your plans for the future

You are now going to read more about what our four friends think about their futures.

Do you remember?

Past: ________ed

Past perfect: have/ had + ________ed

Past continuous: was/were + ________ing

Past perfect continuous: had/ have been + ________ing

Passive: has/have been ________ed

Past continuous passive: was/were being ________ed

Living the dream

PRACTISE

1 Look at the comic strip. Put the verbs in brackets into the past tense. Use the 'Do you remember?' box to help you. Write the sentences into your notebook or on the worksheet provided by your teacher.

2 Now read the next comic strip. Put all the verbs in brackets into the past tense. Use the 'Do you remember?' box to help you. Write the sentences into your notebook or on the worksheet provided by your teacher.

3 Add the correct pronouns from the box to complete this discussion. Write the sentences in your notebook or on the worksheet provided by your teacher.

anything	everyone	something	mine	some	this

4 Use complex noun phrases from the box to complete this discussion. Write the sentences in your notebook or on the worksheet provided by your teacher.

living the dream	in my wildest dreams	my dream job
a very worthwhile profession	a little silly	the hungry and the poor

CHALLENGE YOURSELF

How is your work on your dream board going? Spend some time doing further research now. You have a lot of new language you can use around 'dreams'. Perhaps some of it will be useful on your dream board.

Reading

Read about achieving dreams

1 Read this article about Nancy Roman. Nancy became famous not because she was a movie star but because her achievements were impressive, and unusual for a woman in the mid-twentieth century. As you read, think about the ratings list for Jim Carrey and Maisie Williams on page 144, but this time apply the ratings to achieving success rather than becoming famous. Here are the ratings again – what do you think is most important for achieving your dreams?

- Believing you can do it
- Hard work
- Visualising you can do it
- Good luck

Reach for the stars

You have probably heard of the Hubble Space Telescope, but have you heard of Nancy Roman? This amazing woman is often described as the 'Mother of Hubble' because of her role in developing the Hubble Space Telescope.

Nancy was born in 1925 in the USA and became fascinated by science at a very young age. Both her parents were interested in the natural world and Nancy said that looking up at the clear night skies in Nevada, where she lived, helped fuel her fascination for the stars. When she was eleven, Nancy formed an astronomy club with her school friends. Each week she and her friends learned about the constellations by looking at books. By the time she entered high school, Nancy knew that she wanted to become an astronomer when she grew up, even though this was considered an unusual career for a woman.

Like so many women in the mid-twentieth century, Nancy was dissuaded from a career in science by people around her. One of her teachers said he usually discouraged women from studying physics, although he thought that Nancy 'might make it'. Another teacher thought it was more 'lady-like' to study Latin rather than mathematics. Despite this, Nancy was determined not to be put off her dream career, saying, 'I never seriously considered any occupation other than astronomy.' She eventually obtained a degree in astronomy. After working as a researcher for six years, Nancy was invited to join NASA in 1959. Just six months later, in 1960, she became the first Chief of Astronomy.

Like many women during this era, Nancy found it difficult to obtain recognition for her scientific research, but she never gave up. She was involved in many research projects connected with astronomy, but the biggest of these was the development of a large space telescope. This eventually became the famous Hubble Space Telescope, which gives astronomers – and us – the opportunity to view parts of the universe never seen before.

Although she died in 2018, Nancy's legacy continues. NASA has announced it will name its next-generation space telescope the Nancy Grace Roman Space Telescope, or Roman Space Telescope for short. This telescope will be launching in the 2020s.

2 Answer these questions:
  a Why is Nancy known as the 'Mother of Hubble'?
  b What opinion does the writer express about Nancy in this sentence: *This amazing woman is often described as the 'Mother of Hubble'.*
  c Why did Nancy become interested in astronomy?
  d Did people at the time think this was a good career for a girl?
  e What did Nancy's teacher mean when she said that Latin was more 'lady-like' than mathematics?
  f What did Nancy mean when she said, 'I never seriously considered any occupation other than astronomy'?
  g Is this statement from the text a fact or an opinion? How do you know? *Nancy was invited to join NASA in 1959.*
  h What was Nancy's job at NASA?
  i What is the writer's opinion of the importance of Nancy's work? Find words in the last paragraph that show this.
  j Do you agree that it is important to pursue your dream job, even if your teachers disagree with your choices? Why or why not?

3 Read this short review of *Becoming*, an autobiography by Michelle Obama, and then answer the questions.

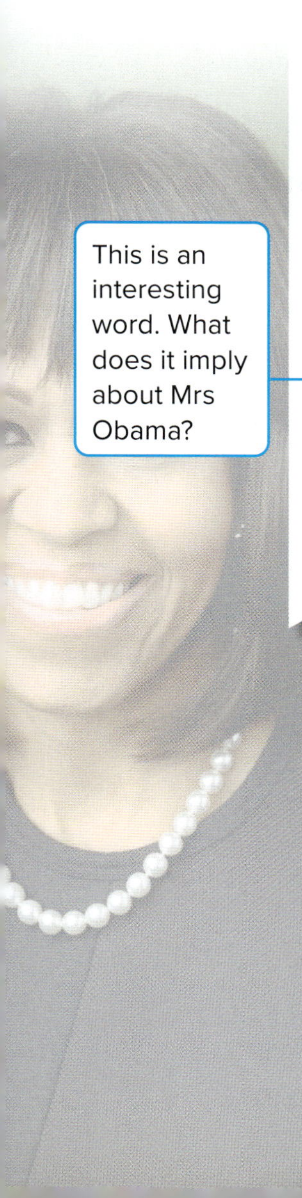

Michelle Obama is one the most famous women of our era. She was the first African American First Lady of the United States of America. She became a powerful advocate for women and girls in the US and around the world. Along the way, she showed us some stylish dressing, and raised two down-to-earth daughters in a very watched and public space.

Look at the adjectives in these sentences. What does that tell you about what the writer thinks of Mrs Obama?

In her memoir, Michelle Obama writes about the experiences that have shaped her – from her childhood on the South Side of Chicago to her years as a lawyer, balancing the demands of motherhood and work. And then, of course, to her time spent at the world's most famous address.

This is an interesting word. What does it imply about Mrs Obama?

She tells her full story as she lived it – in her own words and on her own terms. *Becoming* is the deeply personal story of a woman who inspires us to defy **expectations**, just as she has done.

What does the writer believe about Mrs Obama?

4 Answer these questions.
  a What is the purpose of this piece of writing?
  b How does the writer accomplish her purpose?
  c What picture of Michelle Obama does the information build in your mind?
  d What does the reviewer think of Michelle Obama?
  e Do you think the reviewer is biased in any way? How can you prove this?

Speaking and listening

Dreaming of the future

In this lesson you are going to be sharing your dream boards with your classmates. You will answer questions about your dream board, and also ask questions about other people's dream boards.

1 Look carefully at this dream board that Andy made on Pinterest. Listen to Audio 9.3 as she explains what her dream board means to her.

> **HINT**
> Remember to be sensitive to other people's dreams. Don't laugh at anyone else or make fun of each other. Listen with respect, and ask thoughtful questions.

▲ Andy's dream board

2 Use Andy's dream board to practise asking and answering questions in pairs.
Take turns. First listen to your partner, then ask a question.
- What do you think of …?
- Do you like that idea?
- Does that make sense to you?

If you disagree, be polite. Try these expressions.
- I'm afraid I disagree with you.
- I don't think that …
- Another way to look at it is …

If you are not sure what to say next, try these expressions.
- Let me see.
- The things is …
- Let me think.
- What I mean is …

3 Take turns to present your dream board to the class, and to speak to the class about it.
- Speak slowly and clearly.
- Be enthusiastic about plans which make you happy.
- Allow your classmates to ask three or four questions after you have finished talking.
- Reply to the questions, using the strategies in exercise 2.

Display your dream boards in the classroom, if you have made physical boards.

Hold fast to dreams

LET'S TALK

1 Here are two poems about dreams that were written by different poets, almost a hundred years ago. Read them together in your group.

- a Do you agree with the emotions expressed in the poems?
- b Are these poems still relevant, even though they are very old?
- c Which poem do you prefer, and why?

2 Choose one of the poems to read out loud in your group.

- a Read the poem to yourself.
- b Underline the longer words, mark the syllable stresses and say the words aloud.
- c Mark the words in each phrase that you think should be stressed, to show emotion.
- d Then read the poem out loud.

Dreams

Hold fast to dreams
For if dreams die
Life is a broken-winged bird
That cannot fly.
Hold fast to dreams
For when dreams go
Life is a barren field
Frozen with snow.

– Langston Hughes

HINT

Barren – bare, empty

Embroidered – knitted or decorated

Enwrought – made from, created from

The Cloths of Heaven

Had I the heaven's embroidered cloths,
Enwrought with golden and silver light,
The blue and the dim and the dark cloths
Of night and light and the half-light;
I would spread the cloths under your feet:
But I, being poor, have only my dreams;
I have spread my dreams under your feet;
Tread softly because you tread on my dreams.

– W.B. Yeats

Writing

Back to the future

Try this

1 Write your own poem about your dreams. You can use the poems by Langston Hughes and W.B. Yeats for ideas and inspiration. You could

- compare your dream to something precious (a bird or a cloth of heaven)
- say why it is precious to you
- warn people not to break your precious object/dream
- say how your dream will emerge/flower/come true.

Here's an example.

My dream is like a deep cocoon –
Warm, dry and full of hope.
I feel a surge; protect and spoon,
then rising
burst into
A papermoon.

2 Write a letter to yourself in ten years' time. You can bury it in a time capsule, or hide it in the back of your closet. Tell your older self all you had hoped and planned to achieve once you got to that future age. Follow these steps:

Step 1

Use your dream board as a planning tool. You have done all the research, now you can write it out, and present it to your future self.

Step 2

Use the friendly letter format. If you have forgotten the structure of a friendly letter, go back to Unit 3, page 52.

Step 3

- Address yourself directly: Dear ____________ of the future.
- Use the first paragraph to remind future you where you are now – at Stage 9, age ___________, in ____________ (town), feeling ____________. Say what happened today, to give future you a point of reference.

- Write at least three more paragraphs, about what you hope to achieve in work, in family life and in any other field that is important to you.
- Be kind to your future self. Explain that s/he may have achieved different things, and congratulate him/her on his/her achievements.
- Sign off with love and affection.

Step 4

- Ask a friend to proofread the letter for you, and then correct any mistakes. Write out a neat copy to hand in to your teacher.
- Keep your own copy, in a safe place, to read in the future.

HINT

- Have you used a range of past continuous active forms and passive forms?
- Have you used a range of abstract nouns, compound nouns and complex noun phrases?
- Have you used a wide range of pronouns?

Self check

Use this checklist to self-assess your letter.

	Letter writing skills
	Content is relevant
	Format is appropriate
	Uses appropriate vocabulary
	Uses correct spelling, punctuation and sentence structure
	Uses an informal style of writing, as if to a friend
	Begins and ends correctly

What can you do?

Read and review what you can do.

- I can listen to a discussion among friends, an interview with a psychologist about how to achieve my dreams and a young person discussing their dream board.
- I can talk about my dreams and ambitions for the future.
- I can read about famous people who have achieved their dreams.
- I can write a letter to my future self and a poem about my dreams.
- I can use a range of past continuous active forms and passive forms, a range of abstract nouns, compound nouns and complex noun phrases, and a wide range of pronouns.

Now you have completed Unit 9, you may like to try the Unit 9 online knowledge test if you are using the Boost eBook.

Review Units 7–9

PRACTISE

Use words from the box to complete these sentences.

illegal	determination	headsets	banned	scratch-resistant	trespassing	promise

1 Wireless ____________ were invented to be used by astronauts in space.
2 Do your sunglasses have ____________ lenses?
3 The sign says 'No ____________' so we are not allowed to go in there.
4 You may receive a fine if you take part in an ____________ activity.
5 Many professional sportswomen and men are ____________ from making political statements.
6 You will succeed if you have dreams and lots of ____________.
7 Although this project showed a lot of ____________, it did not achieve what it set out to do.

Try this

Work in pairs and complete the conversation. Use pronouns and connectives from the box.

When you are sure of the correct words, read the conversation aloud. Use the correct intonation as you read the statements, questions and exclamations.

no one	unlike	everyone	you	some	that	so that

Mara: What do you think about the space race?

Mei: It seems like such as a waste of money to me.

Mara: I know what ____________ mean. There is so much poverty in the world.

Mei: And our government need to spend money wisely ____________ they can focus on other priorities, such as climate change.

Mara: Yes, maybe. ____________ you, I don't think it is a waste of money. And wealthy people, like Elon Musk and Richard Branson, should be able to use their money on space exploration.

Mei: No, I don't agree. ____________ should be allowed to travel up into space! Space craft damage the ozone layer around Earth.

Mara: ____________ is true. But think of all the useful things that have been invented for use in space that we now use in our everyday lives.

Mei: Yes, ____________ are useful, like sunglasses and Velcro, but that doesn't make space travel a priority.

Mara: Well, you have a point, but ____________ dreams of being able to go up into space one day – well, I know I do!

PRACTISE

Complete these sentences correctly. You will need to choose the correct words to do this.

1 My parents (used to wear/are used to wear) blazers and ties when they were at school.
2 The trip (had not been/was not been) carefully planned.
3 The astronauts (had been sleeping/have slept) when they were interrupted by a message from the captain.
4 He (has been done/has been doing) some interesting work as a social activist recently.
5 Do you know the name of the space exploration business (who/that) Elon Musk built?
6 The spaceships, (which/who) will carry people, will be used for many trips.
7 Foil blankets (were invented/have invented] by NASA to protect spacecraft and people in space.
8 Why are statues (being removed/have been removed) by government officials?
9 We (have been watching/were watching) the spacecraft take off when suddenly we saw an explosion.
10 (Despite/Although) laws which are designed to protect them, pangolins are still being trafficked.

PRACTISE

Write a paragraph about your dreams for the future.

- Start with a statement about what your dream is.
- Then write four or five sentences to give details about your dream. You can explain it and give reasons to support it.
- Remember to use punctuation to make your information interesting. You can use capital letters, bullet points, colons and brackets – or any other punctuation you think will be useful.

LET'S TALK

Work in small groups. Look at the pictures below and talk about them. Do a short presentation on one of these topics about space travel:

- Why space travel is useful
- Why space travel can fulfil dreams
- Space travel and the movies
- Experiences in space

Make sure your presentation is clear and that you pronounce words clearly. You can use notes on a screen or on a poster to support your presentation.

HINT

Check your paragraph carefully for spelling and language errors.

CHALLENGE YOURSELF

Write a short poem about obeying or not obeying rules.

- Brainstorm some ideas and words.
- Connect the words to make short lines in a poem.

Glossary

activist (noun) someone who believes strongly in a cause and protests about it

addicted (verb) depending on something that is hard to give up

adolescence (noun) the time during which a young person becomes an adult

affect (verb) to make something change

asteroid (noun) a small, rocky, planet-like body that circles the Sun, mostly found between the orbits of Jupiter and Mars. The size of an asteroid can range from less than one mile across to five hundred miles across

atmosphere (noun) the gases surrounding the Earth or other similar objects in outer space

audition (verb) to try out for a part in a play or a show

autobiography (noun) the story of a person's life written or told by that person

barren (adjective) bare

beatboxing (noun) a musical style or technique, especially in hiphop, in which the sounds and rhythms of percussion instruments or a drum machine are simulated by using the mouth and voice

blazer (noun) a sports jacket in a solid, sometimes bright colour, often with a school or club emblem on the breast pocket

blog (noun) shortened from 'Web log', an online journal that may be personal or topical, in which the author makes regular entries that can be read by the general public

cameo (noun) a minor role played by a prominent actor or actress in a single scene of a film

campaign (noun) a series of planned actions carried out in order to reach a particular goal

claustrophobic (adjective) feeling unhappy or fearful of being in a small space and not being able to escape

coin (verb) to make up or invent a new phrase or expression

collision (noun) coming together with force; a crash

commit to (verb) make an agreement or decision to do something and then do it

contradiction (noun) the state of being in denial of or in complete disagreement with something else

cortex *pl cortices* (noun) the outer layer of the cerebellum in the brain

crop yield (noun phrase) the amount of crops produced

cultured meat (noun phrase) meat that is grown from an animal cell, in a laboratory

décor (noun) the way a room is decorated or furnished

detox (noun) a process or period of time in which one abstains from or rids the body of toxic or unhealthy substances; detoxification

distracting (adjective) taking your attention away from something

diverse (adjective) showing a great deal of variety; very different. Often including or involving people from a range of different social and ethnic backgrounds and of different genders, sexual orientations, etc.

draft (verb) drawing up the first version of a piece of writing

eco-tourism (noun) responsible travel to natural areas

effect (noun) the result of a change

efficiently (adverb) in a way that is quick and without making mistakes

effortlessly (adverb) doing something that needs very little physical or mental energy

endangered (adjective) in danger of disappearing (animals and plants)

exceptional (adjective) different, unusual or out of the ordinary

exercises (noun) activity done to keep or make the body or mind strong

expectations (noun) the things people expect you to do

exploit (verb) to use something in a bad way, either to get something you want or to make money

exploration (noun) the act of exploring, investigating or examining

extra-terrestrial (adjective) existing or coming from a place outside planet Earth

fitness (noun) physical condition, especially the condition of one's muscles and heart

food security (noun phrase) having reliable access to enough affordable, nutritious food

frogspawn (noun) the jellylike substance secreted by frogs, that contains the young tadpoles

go viral (phrase) when something is quickly and widely spread through social media

grid (noun) a network of cables or pipes for distributing power, especially high-voltage transmission lines for electricity

gyre (noun) a spiral pattern in the ocean currents

honoured (adjective) respected

illegal (adjective) something that is against the law

impulsive (adjective) doing something without thinking about it first

influencer (noun) a person with the ability to influence potential buyers of a product or service by promoting or recommending the items on social media

inhospitable (adjective) (of an environment) harsh and difficult to live in; (of a person) unfriendly and unwelcoming toward people

inject (verb) to introduce something new

interacting (noun) being and doing something with someone

lobby (noun) a hall or open room inside the entrance of a hotel, theatre, or other large building. It is often used as a waiting room

looting (verb) to openly and forcefully seize goods from a place, often during a war or riot

malnourishment (noun) the lack of enough or appropriate nourishment; malnutrition

mannequin (noun) a model of a human torso or body used to fit or display clothing

mature (adjective) adult, grown up

meaningful (adjective) full of meaning or significance

meditate (verb) to think calmly, deeply and at length, or to clear the mind for a period of time as a way to discipline oneself and find peace

meme (noun) a humorous image, video, piece of text, etc. that is copied (often with slight variations) and spread rapidly by internet users

mindful (adjective) careful; attentive

negatively (adverb) in a way that is bad

nutritious (adjective) having a large amount of vitamins, minerals or other nutrients

orbit (verb) to move in a circle around. For example, the moon orbits Earth

organic (adjective) relating to living matter; produced or producing naturally, without using pesticides or other added chemicals

over-tourism (noun) mass tourism that damages the environment and disturbs the local people

particularly (adverb) to an unusual degree; more than other things in a group

pay attention (verb) to consider or take notice of someone or something; to focus

petition (noun) a formal, written request by many people that is made to a person in authority

podcast (noun) an audio recording that can be downloaded from the internet, usually consisting of a short talk or programme on a particular topic

positively (adverb) in a way that is good

preservative (noun) a substance used to keep foods from going bad or spoiling

protest (noun) an organised public demonstration expressing strong objection to an official policy or course of action

proven (adjective) something that has been shown to be true or correct

quadrangle (noun) large, open, usually grassy area with buildings on all four sides, especially on a college campus; quad

reach (verb) to arrive at or get to a point; to stretch out an arm in order to touch something

regulation (noun) a rule or law that controls or directs people's actions

render (verb) to give or offer, to deliver

reputation (noun) being known for something

rig up (verb) to make, set up or construct something

role model (noun) a person whose actions set an example or are copied by others

romanticise (verb) to think about some things in an unrealistic way in which you make things seem better than they really are

scales (noun) small, hard, thin plates that cover fish, reptiles and certain other animals

sci-fi (noun) shortened form of science fiction; fiction based on imagined future scientific or technological advances and major social or environmental changes, frequently portraying space or time travel and life on other planets

self-sufficient (adjective) relying on yourself and not others for food, power and so on

social media (noun phrase) websites and other applications that enable users to create and share content

subsistence farming (noun phrase) farming at a smaller level, with the aim of supporting yourself and your family

sustainable (adjective) conserving an ecological balance by avoiding depletion of natural resources

tights (noun) a piece of clothing made of tight, stretchy material that covers the legs and hips. Tights are worn for exercise and dancing, or as everyday clothing

trespass (verb) an act of entering the property of another without permission, which is against the law

trilogy (noun) a group of three literary or musical works by one author or composer that are related in sequence, theme or the like

UFO (unidentified flying object) a mysterious object seen in the sky for which, it is claimed, no scientific explanation can be found

vegetarian (adjective) does not contain meat or fish

vegetarian (noun) someone who does not eat meat or fish

visualise (verb) to picture or imagine something in your mind

workout (noun) a period or program of physical exercise

Irregular verb forms

Infinitive	Present participle	Simple past	Past participle
to be	being	was/were	been
to beat	beating	beat	beaten
to become	becoming	became	become
to begin	beginning	began	begun
to bend	bending	bent	bent
to bite	biting	bit	bitten
to bleed	bleeding	bled	bled
to blow	blowing	blew	blown
to break	breaking	broke	broken
to bring	bringing	brought	brought
to build	building	built	built
to burn	burning	burnt, burned	burnt, burned
to buy	buying	bought	bought
to catch	catching	caught	caught
to choose	choosing	chose	chosen
to come	coming	came	come
to cut	cutting	cut	cut
to dig	digging	dug	dug
to draw	drawing	drew	drawn
to do	doing	did	done
to drink	drinking	drank	drunk
to drive	driving	drove	driven
to eat	eating	ate	eaten
to fall	falling	fell	fallen
to feel	feeling	felt	felt
to find	finding	found	found
to fly	flying	flew	flown
to forget	forgetting	forgotten	forgotten
to get	getting	got	got
to give	giving	gave	given
to go	going	went	gone
to grow	growing	grew	grown
to have	having	had	had
to hear	hearing	heard	heard
to hide	hiding	hid	hidden
to hit	hitting	hit	hit
to hold	holding	held	held
to hurt	hurting	hurt	hurt
to keep	keeping	kept	kept
to know	knowing	knew	known
to learn	learning	learned, learnt	learned, learnt

Infinitive	Present participle	Simple past	Past participle
to leave	leaving	left	left
to lend	lending	lent	lent
to let	letting	let	let
to lie	lying	lied	lied
to lie (down)	lying	lay	lain
to light	lighting	lit, lighted	lit, lighted
to lose	losing	lost	lost
to make	making	made	made
to mean	meaning	meant	meant
to meet	meeting	met	met
to pay	paying	paid	paid
to put	putting	put	put
to read	reading	read	read
to ride	riding	rode	ridden
to ring	ringing	rung	rung
to run	running	ran	run
to say	saying	said	said
to see	seeing	saw	seen
to sell	selling	sold	sold
to send	sending	sent	sent
to sew	sewing	sewed	sewn
to show	showing	showed	shown
to shut	shutting	shut	shut
to sing	singing	sang	sung
to sit	sitting	sat	sat
to sleep	sleeping	slept	slept
to slide	sliding	slid	slid
to smell	smelling	smelt, smelled	smelt, smelled
to speak	speaking	spoke	spoken
to spend	spending	spent	spent
to stand	standing	stood	stood
to steal	stealing	stole	stolen
to swim	swimming	swam	swum
to take	taking	took	taken
to teach	teaching	taught	taught
to tell	telling	told	told
to think	thinking	thought	thought
to throw	throwing	threw	thrown
to understand	understanding	understood	understood
to wake (up)	waking	woke	woken
to wear	wearing	wore	worn
to win	winning	won	won
to write	writing	wrote	written

Grammar

Abstract nouns

Abstract nouns describe things that you cannot see, feel or touch, such as ideas and thoughts. For example:

- happiness, fun, achievement

Adjectives

Adjectives describe nouns and pronouns and allow us to make comparisons. Adjectives add colour and interest to a story, so they are very important in storytelling. Adjectives do not agree with the noun or pronoun they describe. They do not have plural forms. For example:

- These are eerie places!
- That is the most beautiful place I have ever visited.
- She is taller than her sister.

We can use adjectives to make comparisons. To compare two things we use the comparative form (+ er).

To compare more than two things, use the superlative form (+ est).

If an adjective has more than three syllables, add 'more' or 'most'. For example:

- beautiful, more beautiful, most beautiful

Some adjectives have irregular comparative and superlative forms: For example:

- good, better, best

We can use adjectives in different ways to make comparisons. For example:

- This year there were twice as many people here today as yesterday.
- That is the best place I have ever visited.
- It is one of the highest mountains in the world.
- Are there more visitors than last year or fewer? There are many more visitors this year.
- Flying is by far the quickest way of getting to the island.

We can form adjectives with the suffixes -ing and -ed. For example:

- interested, interesting

Compound adjectives are made with descriptive words joined by a hyphen. For example:

- a well-known fairy tale
- a life-changing experience

Adverbs

Adverbs modify (tell us more about) verbs, adjectives and other adverbs. Adverbs can be words or phrases. They describe manner, place and time, including indefinite time.

Examples:

- She runs quickly. (manner)
- They live near a big farm. (place)
- We visited her yesterday. (time)
- My family has recently moved to Singapore. They have lived there since 2020. (indefinite time)

You can use adverbs to compare actions. For example:

- high, higher, the highest

If an adverb has more than two syllables, you add 'more' or 'most' to make comparisons.

Adverbial phrases tell you more about a verb, just like adverbs do. They do not have a verb.

Connectives

Connectives link words, clauses, sentences and ideas when we speak and when we write. Connectives also help to put events in sequence. For example:

- before, after, then, while, when

We use connectives to give explanations, examples, reasons and purpose. For example:

- and, because, or, but, although, therefore, so, so that, such, so as

Pronouns can also help to connect ideas because they refer back to nouns.

We can use connectives to contrast or show the difference between ideas. Use words such as but, though, although, while, unlike. For example:

- Most people know the name Tim Berners-Lee but/although/though they think he invented the internet.
- Cleopatra ruled a huge empire but/although/though she was not liked by all.
- While Cleopatra was famous for her beauty, she was also a skilled royal leader.
- Unlike you, I have not seen the film.
- Despite the rules about wearing masks, some people still don't wear one.

Conditional clauses

First conditional

We use the first conditional if there is a very real possibility that something will happen in the future. For example:

- If you arrive late, you will miss the train. (If + present simple tense + will)

We use the second conditional when we want to say the second thing will only happen if the first part of the sentence happens. For example:

- If she spoke German, she would study in Germany. (If + past simple tense + would)

Zero conditional clauses (with 'if')

We use the zero conditional to say things we know are true and to talk about science facts. For example:

- If you heat ice, it melts. (If + present simple = present simple)

Gerunds

Gerunds are action nouns that look like verbs. We form gerunds by adding -ing to a verb stem.

A gerund can be the subject of a sentence. For example:

- Swimming is my passion!

(In this sentence the gerund is before the verb.)

A gerund can be the object of a sentence. For example:

- I have stopped reading the news, because so much of it is fake news!

(In this sentence the gerund is after the verb in the main clause.)

After some verbs we can use an infinitive or a gerund. For example:

- I love acting. I love to act.

The following verbs are always followed by a gerund: enjoy, keep, mind, finish, stop.

You can also use gerunds after prepositions of place and time. For example:

- We need to make a decision before advertising the position.

Infinitives

The infinitive form of a verb is a verb that has 'to' in front of it. For example:

- They want to surf this afternoon.

Modal verbs

Modal verbs are verbs that are added to the main verb to express permission, obligation, advice, possibility or ability. Modal verbs do not change form.

Use the infinitive without 'to' after modal verbs:

- can, could: possibility and ability
- may, might: possibility
- must, have to: obligation
- should: give advice, make suggestions
- must: necessity

- may, can: permission
- can, may: make requests
- can't: prohibition

Nouns

A noun phrase is a group of words (without a verb) that makes sense. You can replace the noun with a noun phrase. For example:

- People in the street were queuing to buy the pizzas.

Compound nouns

Compound nouns consist of two nouns. For example:

- classroom, dishcloth

Abstract nouns

Abstract nouns describe things that you can't see or feel or touch, such as ideas and thoughts. For example:

- happiness, fun, determination

Phrases

A phrase is a group of two or more words, without a verb. We can make noun, adjectival, adverbial and prepositional phrases.

Prepositions

Prepositions describe location, time and direction. For example:

- in, on, under, at, near, towards, off

Prepositional phrases

We can use prepositions before adjectives and nouns in prepositional phrases.

Prepositional phrases start with prepositions and can include nouns and adjectives. For example:

- She left <u>on the fast train</u>.

Dependent phrases

Some phrases depend on certain prepositions for their meanings. We always use these prepositions after certain adjectives or verbs to make phrases with a certain meaning. The words they depend on can be adjectives, nouns or verbs. The preposition 'for' is used after many nouns and adjectives. For example:

- Adnan is quite good <u>at</u> sailing. (after an adjective)
- Here is some information <u>about</u> natural wonders. (after a noun)
- The country is famous <u>for</u> its volcanoes. (after an adjective)

Some prepositions are always used after certain verbs. For example:

- We have often argued <u>about</u> tourism at this natural site.
- The site needs to be protected from <u>pollution</u> and over-tourism.
- Do you believe <u>in</u> stories like that?

Pronouns

Pronouns replace nouns, so you don't have to keep repeating the noun.

- Subject pronouns: I, he, she, it, you, we, they
- Object pronouns: me, him, her, it, you, us, them

Demonstrative pronouns

Demonstrative pronouns point out a specific person or thing or contact between people and things. For example:

- this, that, these, those

Indefinite pronouns

Indefinite pronouns refer to people in a general way. For example:

- some, one, anyone, someone, everyone, no one

Quantitative pronouns

Quantitative pronouns indicate an indefinite quantity. For example:

- some, any, none, one, much, many, little, few

Relative pronouns

Relative pronouns connect clauses in sentences. They can be used with prepositions. For example:

- to whom, from whom, with which, on which, from where

Note: If a word is followed by a noun, it is an adjective, not a pronoun.

Quantifiers

Quantifiers describe quantities. They tell us *how many* or *how much* there is of something.
For example:

- all, some, any, no, less, few, most, both, plenty of, enough

Relative clauses and pronouns

Relative clauses are clauses that begin with relative pronouns such as who, that, which, whom, whose, where and why. These pronouns link the clauses and refer back to the previous clause.

We use 'who' to refer to people.

'Whom' is quite formal. Many people would use 'who' or 'that' in this sentence.

Clauses can be defining or non-defining. You can remove a non-defining clause and the sentence will still make sense. For example:

- This is the house where she used to stay. (defining clause)
- Maria, whom you met last week, is my best friend. (non-defining clause)

Register

Register is using language directly according to who you are speaking or writing to. For example, in a formal register you would write:

- It's impressive what Sean has managed to achieve.

In the less formal, or more casual register, you might write:

- Cool, right?

Reported and direct speech

Direct speech

We use this to quote the actual words that someone spoke. Direct speech is always inside speech marks (' and ').

Reported speech

We use reported speech to say what someone said. In reported speech we change the pronouns, the tense of the main verb, demonstratives and any adverbs of time. The word order changes too.
For example:

	Direct speech	Indirect speech
statement	'I have fish and chips,' said the woman.	The woman said she had fish and chips.
question	'Do you know this word?' the teacher asked.	The teacher asked if I knew that word.
command	'Bring your gym clothes tomorrow,' the captain told us.	The captain told us to bring our gym clothes the next day.

When you need to change direct speech to reported speech, do the following:

- Change the word order.
- Look at the verb tenses. Go back one tense.
- Look at the nouns. Change them to pronouns.
- Look at words that express time and change them if necessary. For example:
  this = that
  now = then
  today = that day

Sentences

Sentences have:

- a subject (the person doing the action)
- a verb (the action).

Most sentences also need:

- an object (the thing the action happens to).

The subject and object of a sentence are usually nouns.

Verbs

Verbs have tenses (such as the simple present tense) and voices (such as the active and passive).

Active and passive voices

We can use the active voice or the passive voice of verbs to describe present, future and past actions.
For example:

Tense	Active voice	Passive voice
Simple present	They play baseball in summer.	Baseball is played in summer.
Simple present continuous	They are playing baseball now.	Baseball is being played now.
Future	They will force us to share the room.	We will be forced to share the room.
Simple past	The visitors enjoyed the meal.	The meal was enjoyed by the visitors.
Simple past continuous	The visitors were enjoying a meal when the lights went off.	A meal was being enjoyed by the visitors when the lights went off.
Perfect	Mara has done research for her project.	Research for the project has been done by Mara.

To form the passive, use the verb 'to be' in different tenses + past participle.

To form the passive in a continuous tense, use 'to be' + being + past participle.

Remember that some past participles are irregular. See the list on pages 159–160.

The passive voice is used:
- when you don't need to say who does the action
- if you don't want to say who the subject is.

Verb tenses

Future forms

There are different future forms:

To describe plans and arrangements that have already been made. For example:
- We are going to visit friends this evening. (use going to + verb stem)

To make predictions. For example:
- The sport will appeal to young people.
- I shall be famous one day! (use will/shall + verb stem)

To describe future arrangements with fixed dates. For example:
- The new school year starts on 7 September. (use the present tense)

Past continuous tense

We use this tense to describe an action that was in progress while something else was happening. For example:
- As I was getting on the train, I dropped my phone.

To form this tense: verb 'to be' in the past form (was, were) + present participle (-ing).

Past perfect continuous tense

We use this tense to describe an action that was in progress when something else happened. For example:
- I had been watching the Star Trek movies again, when the TV station stopped showing them.

To form this tense: use had/have been + present participle (-ing).

Past perfect tense

We use this tense to describe an action in the past that was completed before another action in the past. (Use the past perfect to describe the earlier action and the simple past to describe the other, later action.)

To form this tense: use had/has been + the past participle (-ed).

Past simple tense

We usually form the simple past tense -ed.
For example:

- play = played
- dance = danced

Some past tense verbs have irregular past tense forms. For example:

- go = went
- take = took

Look at the list of irregular past tense verbs on pages 159–160 if you are not sure.

Present continuous tense

We use this tense to say what is happening at the moment, as we are speaking. For example:

- I am watching the other passengers on the train.

We also use this tense to talk about future arrangements. For example:

- We are going to Prague next month.

To form this tense: verb 'to be' (am, is, are) + present participle (-ing).

Present perfect tense

We use this tense to describe a recent or unfinished action that we did in the past and that we are still doing or hope to do in the future.

To form this tense: use the verb 'have/has' + past participle.

Present perfect continuous tense

We use this tense:

- to describe something started earlier and is continuing in the present time
- to emphasise the duration of something.

To form this tense: use have/has been + the present participle (-ing).

To form a question: change the word order.

To form a negative: add 'not' after the word 'have'. For example:

- I have not been working.

Remember that if a verb ends in -e, you have to drop the -e before you add -ing.

Present simple tense

We use the present simple tense:

- to talk about habits and routines
- to describe people
- to talk about things that are always true.

For example:

- He/she wears school uniform.

The verb for the third person singular ends in -s.

Punctuation

A B C	Capital letters are used for the first letter of a name, country, place, nationality, days of the week, months of the year or language. Capital letters are also used to start sentences.
.	A full stop shows the end of a sentence. It may also be used after initials, e.g. N.J. Hill and abbreviations, e.g. B.B.C.
,	A comma shows a short pause that separates parts of a sentence or words in a list.
( )	Brackets show extra information or an explanation which is considered less important.
“ ” or ‘ ’	Speech marks show words that are spoken directly. They are also used around the title of films and books. Speech marks may be double – “ ” or single – ‘ ’.
’	An apostrophe is used to replace a letter when two words are contracted , e.g. it is – it’s. An apostrophe is also used to show possession, e.g. Adnan's bicycle – the bicycle belonging to Adnan. It is also used to show possession, e.g. it’s Bill’s.
-	A hyphen is used when two words such as compound nouns are joined together, e.g. son-in-law. It is also used to add extra information in a sentence.
?	A question mark is used at the end of a sentence which asks a direct question. It is also used for requests. Can you buy some milk, please? Should I complete this task now?
:	A colon is used to show that something is coming next, e.g. a list.

Pronunciation

ability
accommodated
accommodation
activists
addicted
adolescence
adulthood
Africa
African American
agenda
agriculture
algae
alien
ambition
anecdote
Antarctica
archaeological site
architect
artificial
ascend
Asia
asteroid
astronauts
astrophysics
athletes
attitude
audience
Australia
autobiography
bacteria
balance
Bali
banana trees
Barack Obama
battling
Belgium
biased
biological
bioreactor
blazer
blurred
boxing
brain
breathe
broadcast
broccoli
brochure
brotherhood
brownies
bucket
bugs
burger patty
camel caravan
camera
campaign
Canada
carbohydrate
cartoon
casualties
cathedral
celebrity chef
cells
centuries
ceramic
challenge
chapatis
cheese
cheque
Chicago
childhood
chilli
China
city council
closed-circuit television
coconut milk
Cold War
collision
Colombia

community
concept
contradict
copper mining
countdown
courtyard
couscous
crest
crickets
crisis
critic
croissants
cruise trip
cucumber
cultivating
cultured
cupcake
cycling
Dalai Lama
dangling
declutter
deduction
defy
deliberately
delicious
depressed
descend
deteriorated

detox
diet
discipline
disgusting
disobey
diverse
doubt
drought
eco-lodge
economy
eco-tourist
efficiently
effortlessly
Eiffel Tower
electricity
electronic
Ellen DeGeneres
Elon Musk
engineering
enthusiasm
entrepreneur
Ethiopia
Europe
exchange
exhausted
expectations
exploit
exploration

explorers
extra-terrestrial
farmers
fascinating
fashion
fertiliser
fibre
fields
fitness coach
flexibility
flight
float
foil blanket
food security
food strikes
freeze-dried food
frogspawn
funeral
funnelled
Galapagos Islands
garbage
gas-guzzling
generator
glory
gorilla
government
groan
gym

healthy
hillside
holy
honesty
Hubble Space Telescope
humidity
hydrated
iceberg
ignition
ignore
illegal
inadequate
India
Indonesia
influencer
influential
ingredients
injera bread
injuries
injustice
insects
insomnia
Instagram
integrity
Irish stew
Jamaica
Japan
jewellery
Jim Carrey
Joe Wicks
joggers
joke
Jordanian desert
Kerala
laboratory
launch
lawyer
lenses
lifestyle
limbs
London
looters
Lost City
lyrics
Maddy Moate
magazine
Maisie Williams
maize
malaria
marches
Mars
marvellous
mature
mayor
meat
meditating
meme
merchants
methane
Michael Jordan
Michelle Obama
mindfulness
minerals
miserable
molecules
mountainside
movie star
mules
muscle
museum
naan
Nancy Roman
negative
newspaper
noticeboard
off-grid
opinion
Oprah Winfrey
orbit
organic
Pacific Ocean
packaging
pangolins
paradise

Parc des Volcans
Paris
parkour
participants
peer
petitions
pilgrims
Pinterest
plank
plastic
plight
podcast
police
pollution
president
prison
profession
professor
protein
protest
pulleys
punish
purify
quadrangle
reclaim
recycling
refreshments
refugees
repellent
respectful
restaurant
Rhianna
Richard Branson
risk-taking
rite of passage
robotic
rocket
romanticise
ropes
ruins
Russia
Rwanda
San Francisco
sand dunes
sarcastic
satchels
sceptic
scheme
scientist
scoop
sea turtle
seaweed
self-sufficient
servants
shallow
shock-absorbers
Sierra Leone
Sierra Nevada
Silk Route
slang
slope
small-scale
snag
solar panels
space
spaghetti
speculation
spiritual
sponsored
squat
Star Wars
statue
stealing
sterile
stressful
stretch
struggle
subsistence farmers
sunglasses
supplement
sustainable
sweltering
tadpoles
Taylor Swift

teenagers
temper
temperature
terrace
Thai
The Netherlands
thermometer
tie
tights
TikTok
tourism
toxic
treadmill
trespass
tribe
trilogy
tropical
vegetarian
Vietnam
viral
visualise
vitamins
wealthy
wildlife
wisdom
wooden
workout
World Bank
Yemeni
yoga
YouTube
yuck

Reading for enjoyment

Do you want to find out more about some of the topics you have learned about? Reading a range of fiction and non-fiction books for enjoyment will help build up your vocabulary in English. Use a dictionary to look up some words you don't know, but remember you don't have to look up every word you're not sure about because you can try and work it out from the context. It's a good idea to keep a reading journal, so you can record what you have read and what you thought about the book.

Here are some suggested fiction and non-fiction books you might like to try.

Third-party resources referred to in this section have not been endorsed by Cambridge Assessment International Education.

Winterborne Home for Vengeance and Valour (ISBN: 9781408357378) by Ally Carter, Orchard Books

Planet Omar: Accidental Trouble Magnet (ISBN: 9781444951226) by Zanib Mian, Hodder Children's Books

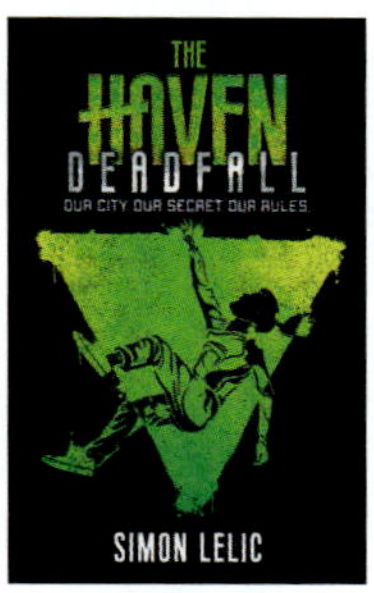

Deadfall: Book 3 (The Haven) (ISBN: 9781444947649) by Simon Lelic, Hodder Children's Books

My Awesome Guide to Getting Good at Stuff (ISBN: 9781526362681) by Matthew Syed, Wren & Rook

Go Big: The Secondary School Survival Guide (ISBN: 9781526362353) by Matthew Burton, Wren & Rook

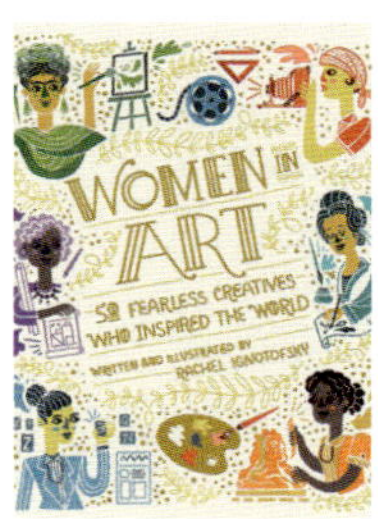

Women in Art: 50 Fearless Creatives Who Inspired the World (ISBN: 9781526362452) by Rachel Ignotofsky, Wren & Rook

Toto the Ninja Cat and the Great Snake Escape (ISBN: 9781444939453) by Dermot O'Leary, Hodder Children's Books

The Paper & Hearts Society Book 1: Find Your People (ISBN: 9781444949247) by Lucy Powrie, Hodder Children's Books

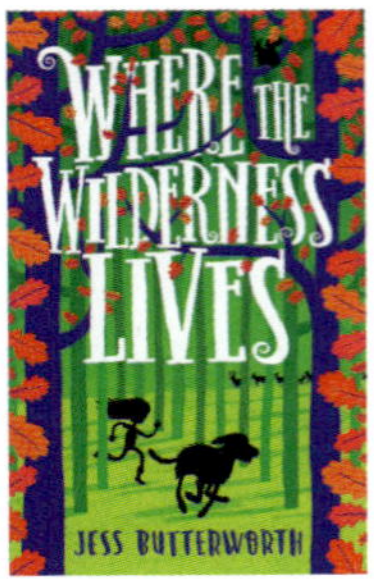

Where the Wilderness Lives (ISBN: 9781510105508) by Jess Butterworth, Orion Children's Books

Fire Boy (ISBN: 9781444954685) by J M Joseph, Hodder Children's Books

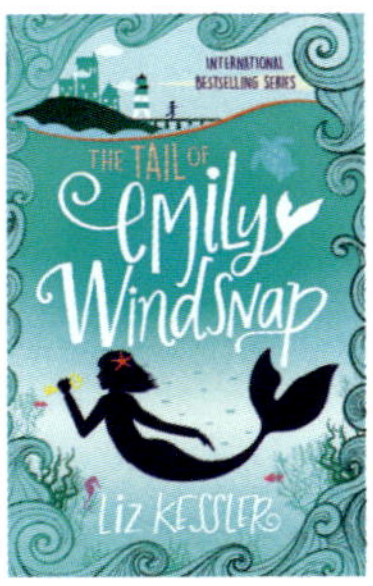

The Tail of Emily Windsnap (ISBN: 9781444015096) by Liz Kessler, Orion Children's Books

Find Your Girl Squad (ISBN: 9781526362506) by Dr Angharad Rudkin and Ruth Fitzgerald, Wren & Rook

The Boy at the Back of the Class (ISBN: 9781510105010) by Onjali Q Rauf, Orion Children's Books

This Book Will (Help) Cool the Climate (ISBN: 9781526362414) by Isabel Thomas, Wren & Rook

Boot: Small Robot, Big Adventure (ISBN: 9781444949360) by Shane Hegarty, Hodder Children's Books

Secrets in the Skies (ISBN: 9781526360014) by Giles Sparrow, Wren & Rook

Engineering Power! Machines in Space (ISBN: 9781526311801) by Kay Barnham, Wayland

Stand Against: Prejudice (ISBN: 9781445168210) by Izzi Howell, Franklin Watts

Animals in Disguise (ISBN: 9781526312143) by Michael Bright, Wayland

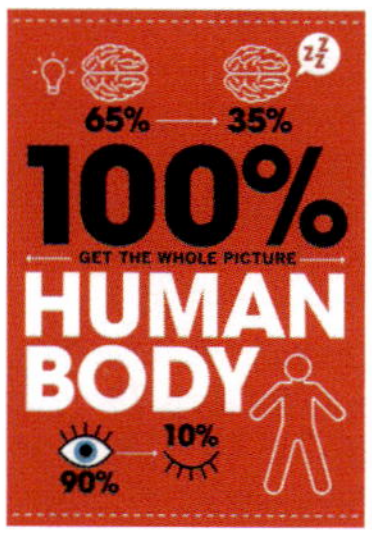

100% Get the Whole Picture: Human Body (ISBN: 9781526308139) by Paul Mason, Wayland

Stand Against: Poverty and Hunger (ISBN: 9781445167398) by Alice Harman, Franklin Watts

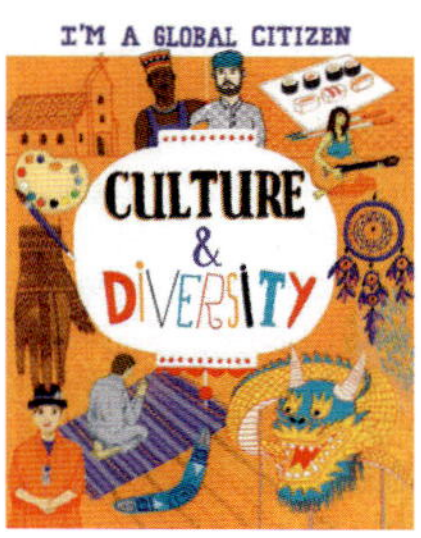

I'm a Global Citizen: Culture and Diversity (ISBN: 9781445163987) by Georgia Amson-Bradshaw, Franklin Watts

Space Science: STEM in Space: Science for Rocketing into Space (ISBN: 9781526308115) by Mark Thompson, Wayland

Space Science: STEM in Space: Science for Exploring Outer Space (ISBN: 9781526308467) by Mark Thompson, Wayland

Cats React to Science Facts (ISBN: 9781526311160) by Izzi Howell, Scholastic Inc.

Endangered Wildlife: Ocean Life (ISBN: 9781526310002) by Anita Ganeri, Wayland

Acknowledgements

r = right, *l* = left, *b* = bottom, *t* = top, *m* = middle

Text credits

p.8 'How Teenage Sisters Pushed Bali To Say "Bye-Bye" To Plastic Bags' by Michael Sullivan, January 26, 2019, © NPR; **p.17** '"They just wanted us to read about a white boy and his dog": why teenager Marley Dias fought back' by Coco Khan, 28 August 2019, © *Guardian News & Media Limited*; **p.33** 'Colombia's "Lost City" is older than Machu Picchu, and hardly anyone visits' by Emily Gillespie, 20th June 2019, © Cable News Network; **pp.48–49** 'What teenage brains can teach us about thinking creatively' By Steven Johnson, March 4, 2020, © *The Washington Post*; **pp.94–95** 'Teenager's collection of 37,000 tadpoles turns her into a TikTok star' by Elle Hunt, 7 July 2020, © *Guardian News & Media Limited*; **p.98** Hani Sidow, Instagram handle @Hanihanss; **p.99** 'About us: Our Community' © Self-Care Is For Everyone; **p.100** *t* © Maddie Moat/Mirador Management; **p.100** *b* © Charli D'Amelio LLC; **p.102** © Lionel the Hog; **p.151** *t* Langston Hughes, 'Dreams' from *The Collected Works of Langston Hughes*. Copyright © 2002 by Langston Hughes. Reprinted by permission of David Higham Associates Limited. All rights reserved.

Photo credits

p.6 *l* © WENN Rights Ltd/Alamy Stock Photo; *r* © John Lamparski/WireImage/Getty Images; **p.8** *t* © David Pereiras/stock.adobe.com; *b* © World of Marie; **p.9** © David Pereiras/stock.adobe.com; **p.10** *t* © John Lamparski/WireImage/Getty Images; *b* © Hroephoto/stock.adobe.com; **p.11** © Hroephoto/stock.adobe.com; **p.12** *t* © Joanne Dale/stock.adobe.com; **p.12** *b* © Astrid Stawiarz/Shorty Awards/Getty Images; **p.12** *b m* © Mari Copeny; **p.12** *b r* © Mari Copeny **p.13** © Joanne Dale/stock.adobe.com; **p.15** © Alphaspirit/stock.adobe.com; **p.17** © WENN Rights Ltd/Alamy Stock Photo; **p.18** *t* © Pro_Vector/stock.adobe.com; **p.18** *m l* © Clement Rossignol/Reuters/Alamy Stock Photo; *m* © The Ocean Cleanup; *r* © Frans Blok/Shutterstock.com; **p.19** © Frans Blok/Shutterstock.com; **p.20** *t* © Metamorworks/stock.adobe.com; *b* © Mix and Match Studio/stock.adobe.com; **p.21** © Mix and Match Studio/stock.adobe.com; **p.22** *t* © Mangostock/stock.adobe.com; *b* © Karl Allen Lugmayer/Shutterstock.com; **p.23** *t* © Can/stock.adobe.com; *b* © Karl Allen Lugmayer/Shutterstock.com; *m* © Yotrakbutda/stock.adobe.com; **p.25** *t* © Grant Tiffen/stock.adobe.com; *b* © Longjourneys/stock.adobe.com; **p.27** © Robert/stock.adobe.com; **p.29** © Amar Grover/John Warburton-Lee Photography/Alamy Stock Photo; **p.30** © Vladimir Wrangel/stock.adobe.com; **p.32** © David/stock.adobe.com; **p.33** © Scottiebumich/stock.adobe.com; **p.34** © JoergSteber/stock.adobe.com; **p.35** *b* © JoergSteber/stock.adobe.com; **p.35** *t* © Quinn Zeda/Shutterstock.com; **p.36** © F.C.G./stock.adobe.com; **p.37** © Redpixel/stock.adobe.com; **p.38** *t l* © JackF/stock.adobe.com; *t r* © Pathdoc/stock.adobe.com; *b* © Rawpixel.com/stock.adobe.com; **p.40** © Ken McKay/ITV/Shutterstock; **p.41** *l* © Denisismagilov/stock.adobe.com; *r* © Benjavisa Ruangvaree/stock.adobe.com; **p.43** © Baranq/stock.adobe.com; **p.44** © MarekPhotoDesign.com/stock.adobe.com; **p.45** © AndreaObzerova/stock.adobe.com; **p.46** © Solid photos/stock.adobe.com; **p.48** *t* © Mykhailo/stock.adobe.com; *b* © Victor Tongdee/stock.adobe.com; **p. 49** © Victor Tongdee/stock.adobe.com; **p.50** © Mykhailo/stock.adobe.com; **p.51** © 1STunningART/stock.adobe.com; **p.52** © Prostock-studio/stock.adobe.com; **p.55** *l* © Yotrakbutda/stock.adobe.com; *r* © Stu Shaw/Shutterstock.com; **p.56** *t l* © Robynmac/stock.adobe.com; *t r* © Lindahughes/stock.adobe.com; *b l* © Arundhati/stock.adobe.com; *b r* © Nerudol/stock.adobe.com; **p.59** © Saburou/stock.adobe.com; **p.62** *t* © Hquality/stock.adobe.com; **p.62** © Hao Zhou/stock.adobe.com; **p.63** © Hao Zhou/stock.adobe.com; **p.64** © Jiri Hera/stock.adobe.com; **p.65** © Weerapat1003/stock.adobe.com; **p.57** *m l* © Iryna/stock.adobe.com; *m r* © Aysu/stock.adobe.com; *l* © Rawpixel.com/stock.adobe.com; *r* © Fotodesign-jegg.de/stock.adobe.com; **p.66** *l* © Iryna/stock.adobe.com; *m l* © Aysu/stock.adobe.com; *m r* © Rawpixel.com/stock.adobe.com; *r* © Fotodesign-jegg.de/stock.adobe.com; **p.68** © PixAchi/stock.adobe.com; **p.69** © Marcos/stock.adobe.com; **p.70** © Delicious/stock.adobe.com; **p.71** © CK Bangkok Photo/stock.adobe.com; **p.72** *t l* © IHX/stock.adobe.com; *t r* © David/stock.adobe.com; *b l* © M-SUR/stock.adobe.com; *b r* © F Armstrong Photography/Shutterstock.com; **pp.73–75** © Knssr/stock.adobe.com; **p.76** © Sirikorn/stock.adobe.com; **p.77** © Ananaline/stock.adobe.com; **p.78** *t* © John Roche/Shutterstock.com; *b* © Aleksej/stock.adobe.com; **p.82** *l* © Damien/stock.adobe.com; *r* © HollyHarry/stock.adobe.com; **p.83** © Damien/stock.adobe.com; **p.85** © Janne/stock.adobe.com; **p.86** *l* © Aheflin/stock.adobe.com; *m* © Eray Uman/Shutterstock.com; *r* © Andrew/stock.adobe.com; **p.87** © Aheflin/stock.adobe.com; **p.88** *t* © AFF-USA/Shutterstock; *b* © Amenic181/stock.adobe.com; **p.89** © Highwaystarz/stock.adobe.com; **p.91** © Jon Kopaloff/Getty Images; **p.94** © Paul McErlane/Guardian News & Media Ltd 2021; **p.98** © Hani Sidow, Instagram handle @Hanihanss; **p.99** *t* © Jordan Strauss/Invision/AP/Shutterstock; *b* © WHAT.IS.MENTAL.ILLNESS; **p.100** *t* © Owen James Vincent; *b* © Jacopo Raule/WireImage/Getty Images; **p.104** © Sergey Nivens/stock.adobe.com; **p.105** © Sergey Nivens/stock.adobe.com; **p.106** © Wowinside/stock.adobe.com; **p.107** © Alonesdj/stock.adobe.com; **p.108** *b m l* © Roman Samokhin/stock.adobe.com; *b m r* © Pixelrobot/stock.adobe.com; *t l* © 279photo/stock.adobe.com; *t m l* © Vladislav Ociacia/stock.adobe.com; *b l* © PaulPaladin/stock.adobe.com; *b r* © Nazarovsergey/stock.adobe.com; *t m r* © Sportpoint/stock.adobe.com; *t r* © Goir/stock.adobe.com; *t l* © Nejron Photo/stock.adobe.com; *t m l* © Chukov/stock.adobe.com; *t m r* © Alexander Lutsenko/stock.adobe.com; *t r* © Sergey/stock.adobe.com; *b l* © Mylips/stock.adobe.com; *b m l* © Kuchina/stock.adobe.com; *b m r* © Sumrith/stock.adobe.com; *b r* © Fabian/stock.adobe.com; **p.110** © NASA; **p.111** *t* © NASA; *b* © NASA; **p.112** *t* © Paopano/stock.adobe.com; *b* © Ustas/stock.adobe.com; **p.113** © NASA/Clouds AO/SEArch; **p.115** © NASA; **p.116** © Forestgraphic/stock.adobe.com; **p.117** © Forestgraphic/stock.adobe.com; **p.118** © European Southern Observatory/M. Kornmesser; **p.119** © Magann/stock.adobe.comp. **p.120** © Grandfailure/stock.adobe.com; **p.121** © Grandfailure/stock.adobe.com; **p.122** *t l* © Koldunova_anna/stock.adobe.com; *t r* © Ake1150/stock.adobe.com; *b r* © Dragana Gordic/stock.adobe.com; *b r* © Brandon Klein/stock.adobe.com; **p.125** © Rawpixel.com/stock.adoebe.com; **p.127** *l* © Monkey Business/stock.adobe.com; *r* © Pixel-Shot1/stock.adobe.com; **p.128** © Charoenchai/stock.adobe.com; **p.129** © Standret/stock.adobe.com; **p.130** © Charoenchai/stock.adobe.com; **p.133** © IanDagnall Computing/Alamy Stock Photo; **p.134** © Dampoint/stock.adobe.com; **p.136** *t* © Chrispo/stock.adobe.com; *b* © EvgeniyBobrov/stock.adobe.com; **p.138** *t l* © Oneinchpunch/stock.adobe.com; *t r* © Dimazel/stock.adobe.com; *b l* © Rawpixel.com/stock.adobe.com; *b r* © GuruXOX/stock.adobe.com; **p.139** *l* © Iryna/stock.adobe.com; *m l* © Aysu/stock.adobe.com; *m r* © Rawpixel.com/stock.adobe.com; *r* © Fotodesign-jegg.de/stock.adobe.com; **p.140** © Three Sixty Images/Shutterstock.com; **p.141** *l* © lev radin/Shutterstock.com; *r* © Bruce Cotler/Globe Photos/ZUMA Press, Inc/Alamy Stock Photo; **p.142** © Sergey Nivens/stock.adobe.com; **p.143** © CD_PIX/stock.adobe.com; **p.144** © Anton Ivanov/Shutterstock.com; **p.145** © Eversummerphoto/Shutterstock.com; **p.148** *r* © NASA Archive/Alamy Stock Photo; *l* © NASA/Agefotostock/Alamy Stock Photo; **p.149** © White House Photo/Alamy Stock Photo; **p.151** t © Dan Kosmayer/stock.adobe.com; *b* © Marinakutukova/stock.adobe.com; **p.152** © Romolo Tavani/stock.adobe.com; **p.155** *l* © Dimazel/stock.adobe.com; *r* © DGIM studio/stock.adobe.com